CONTENTS

This student lecture companion was prepared by Barbara St. John, RN, PhD, assistant professor of nursing at Western Carolina University. Barbara has taught nursing for seven years at the associate, baccalaureate, and master's levels. She currently teaches community health nursing, nursing theory, and patient education. Barbara was a teacher before she became a nurse, and believes that patient education is a unique aspect of all nursing practice.

CHAPTER 1

Overview of Education in Health Care

Critical Thinking

A. Chapter Summary: Write two or three sentences on what you understand to be the main idea(s) of Chapter 1:

_____

_____

_____

_____

_____

_____

_____

B. Debate: The following definition of the educational process emphasizes the role of both teacher and learner. Do you agree or disagree with the statement that the outcome of the educational process includes growth in the teacher as well as the learner? Defend your position.

> The educational process is a systematic, sequential, planned course of action consisting of two major interdependent operations, teaching and learning. This process forms a continuous cycle that also involves two interdependent players, the teacher and the learner. Together, they jointly perform teaching and learning activities, the outcome of which leads to mutually desired behavior changes. These changes foster growth in the learner and, it should be acknowledged, growth in the teacher as well. (p. 10)

Small Group Discussion

Share an experience from your personal or professional background (as patient or educator) that involved the failure of the patient education process. Why do you think this happened?

Case Study

After reading this case study, answer the questions that follow.

A small military hospital at an isolated duty station in California relied on registered nurse volunteers with the American Red Cross to teach patient education classes. One of the classes was called the "Early Bird Class" for women with newly diagnosed pregnancies. The class was mandatory in order to get an initial prenatal appointment whether this was a first pregnancy or not. Both active duty women and wives of military personnel were required to attend the class. Numbers at the class were usually high—the weekly audience varied from 5 to 20 women.

The small classroom was located at the base's chapel, and was used for Sunday School on weekends. Due to budget cutbacks, most materials for teaching were over five years old or home-made. They consisted of a brief video on early pregnancy, lectures with flip charts, and handouts. The audio-visual equipment was unreliable.

Some of the topics covered were nutrition, avoidance of alcohol and tobacco, exercise guidelines, management of discomforts, what to expect from the hospital's prenatal care and delivery processes, signs and symptoms of prenatal emergencies, and information on other preparation for childbirth classes. While some patients voiced resentment or frustration at their required attendance, the instructor received positive feedback from the hospital staff about the high level of preparedness of these patients.

A. List the barriers to education and the obstacles to learning within this class.

_____

_____

_____

_____

_____

_____

_____

B. The "Early Bird Class" was shown

_____

_____

_____

_____

_____

_____

_____

Links

The March of Dimes Web site aims to improve the health of mothers and babies through patient education. Their Web site offers professionally reviewed materials for both educators and parents as well as support groups and question-and-answer forums.

http://www.marchofdimes.com/professionals/684.asp

This article discusses parental expectations and ways to improve prenatal teaching:

Robertson, A. (2001). Prenatal education . . . time to lift our game. *The Practising Midwife*, 4(1), np. Available at:

http://www.acegraphics.com.au/articles/andrea18.html

CHAPTER 2

Ethical, Legal, and Economic Foundations of the Educational Process

Critical Thinking

A. Chapter Summary: Write two or three sentences on what you understand to be the main idea(s) of Chapter 2:

_____

_____

_____

_____

_____

_____

_____

B. Debate: Consult pp. 26–7 for the text's discussion of patient education and its relationship to informed consent. Do you agree or disagree with the following statement? Defend your position.

> Patients will never be able to give true informed consent for complicated procedures, since concepts such as the relative risk of bad outcomes are difficult for many to fully understand.

Small Group Discussion

What are the provisions in *The Patient's Bill of Rights* related to patient education and informed consent? How are these provisions implemented in your health care facility? Can you think of ways that this implementation could be improved?

Case Study

After reading the following research study abstract, answer the questions that follow.

Hartmann, C. W., Maio, V., Goldfarb, N. I., Cobb, N., Nash, D. B. (2005). Asthma Management Programs in Managed Care Organizations. *Disease Management, 8*(6), 339–45.

The aim of this work was to investigate how managed care organizations (MCOs) currently approach asthma treatment and management and to determine factors affecting asthma outcomes. A Web-based survey was administered to a national sample of 351 medical directors of MCOs to investigate the asthma management program components in their organizations as well as gaps and barriers in the management of patients with asthma. All 134 (38.2%) responding medical directors reported that their organizations monitor asthma patients. Plans use a variety of asthma management activities, including general member education (90%), member education by mail (87%), self-management education (85%), and provider education (82%). Educational resources (89%) and telephone advice nurses (77%) were the most common self-management strategies offered. Among factors impeding the provision of effective asthma care, noncompliance with asthma treatment, the inappropriate use of medications, and the need for multiple medications were cited by virtually all respondents. Health plans rely on an array of strategies to manage asthma patients. Education encouraging patient self-management is a key component of asthma management programs. However, a considerable number of treatment approach barriers are impeding the achievement of proper asthma care. Without innovative approaches to care, it appears that current MCOs' asthma management efforts may not result in substantial improvements in asthma outcomes.

A. What factors do you think prevent individual health care providers from engaging in health promotion activities even when these activities are supported by the managed care system in which they practice?

_____

_____

_____

_____

_____

_____

_____

B. Do you think the study results would have been different if the primary care providers had answered the survey questions instead of the medical directors? If the patients had answered the survey questions?

_____

_____

_____

_____

_____

_____

_____

C. Does this survey address the quality or effectiveness of care provided?

_____

_____

_____

_____

_____

_____

_____

Links

The Web site of the American Society of Anesthesiologists contains extensive materials, videos, PowerPoint shows, brochures, checklists and FAQs designed for direct patient use and for the use of health care professionals engaged in peri-operative patient education. The goal of this organization is "to help you become a more informed patient about the medical care you receive before, during and following surgical and diagnostic procedures."

http://www.asahq.org/patientEducation.htm

"Informed Consent in Research" is a PowerPoint presentation from the Department of Biomedical Engineering at the University of Texas at Austin.

http://www.bme.utexas.edu/igert/IGERT%20krishEthics.ppt

CHAPTER 3

Applying Learning Theories to Healthcare Practice

Critical Thinking

A. Chapter Summary: Write two or three sentences on what you understand to be the main idea(s) of Chapter 3:

_____

_____

_____

_____

_____

_____

_____

B. Debate: In your opinion, which of the following applications of learning theory is the most critical to ensure a good "fit" with a health promotion campaign, (a) assessing the learning styles of the participants, (b) developing goals for behavior or (c) choosing appropriate activities/interventions? Defend your position.

Small Group Discussion

In your personal life, you may have an unhealthy behavior that you have had difficulty changing (smoking, snacking, etc.) or a healthy behavior that you have had difficulty adopting (regular exercise, flossing your teeth). Which learning theory (or theories) might help you with this situation?

Case Study: Employee Health Promotion

A community college has established a Fit and Well for Life (FWL) Committee. The committee is considering adopting the "Dump the Plump" Campaign as its first campaign to promote a healthier lifestyle for its faculty and employees. Teams of 4–10 participants are formed. Each team member sets their own personal weight loss goal for the end of the eight-week campaign, and the personal goals are totaled into a team goal. No more than 50% of each team may have goals of five pounds or less. Twenty minutes of moderate physical activity (walking, swimming, etc.) should be performed six times per week. No special diet is prescribed, but healthy eating tips are promoted regularly. Teams will be judged at the end of the campaign according to the progress they have made towards their goal. Appropriate prizes are awarded to the top three teams.

A. After reading this case study, critique this health promotion campaign choice according to the "Common Principles of Learning" on pp. 67–8. List at least three positive and at least three negative aspects of this campaign according to these principles.

_____

_____

_____

_____

_____

_____

_____

The following year, the FWL Committee chooses the "One Hundred Miles in One Hundred Days" campaign. Participants commit themselves individually to perform moderate-to-vigorous physical activity daily. A variety of acceptable activities are promoted as the equivalent of walking or running one mile a day (20 minutes of swimming, dancing, biking, etc.). Weekly logs are submitted to a department captain. The first three individuals who achieve this are awarded appropriate prizes.

B. Critique this health promotion campaign according to the "Common Principles of Learning" on pp. 67–8 as above. Is the "One Hundred Miles in One Hundred Days" campaign an improvement on the "Dump the Plump" campaign?

_____

_____

_____

_____

_____

_____

C. What advice would you give the FWL Committee based on your analysis of these two campaigns?

_____

_____

_____

_____

_____

_____

_____

Links

National Cancer Institute provides an extensive discussion of health promotion theory at this Web site. Individual theorists are presented. Use the menu on the left of the site to navigate to various sections of interest.

http://cancer.gov/cancerinformation/theory-at-a-glance

Short video with Dr. Bandura (Social Cognitive Theory):

http://video.google.com/videoplay?docid=-2953790276071699877

Determinants of Learning

Critical Thinking

A. Chapter Summary: Write two or three sentences on what you understand to be the main idea(s) of Chapter 4:

_____

_____

_____

_____

_____

_____

_____

B. Debate: Do you agree or disagree with the following statement? Defend your position.

Education in and of itself is not always the answer to a problem. Often, healthcare providers believe that more education is necessary when something goes wrong, when something is not being done, when a patient is not following a prescribed regimen, or when a staff member does not adhere to a protocol. In such instances, always look for other needs which are nonlearning. (p. 80)

Small Group Discussion

Review Learning Style Principle #2. "Teachers need to guard against teaching by their own preferred learning styles." (p. 94). What teaching mode do you tend to rely on most? How do you tend to learn the best? Is there a similarity between the two styles? See links on p. 15 for two self-assessments of learning style.

Case Study

After reading this case study, complete the exercises that follow.

Mr. T.Y. is a 51-year-old Caucasian male scheduled for cardiac catheterization. His risk factors for heart disease are prior congestive heart disease, transient ischemic attack involving left arm, former prolonged tobacco use, a diet high in saturated fat, hyperlipidemia, obesity, hypertension, and poorly controlled diabetes. He made some attempts at risk reduction, stopping smoking two years ago and losing 40 pounds. However, he currently enjoys eating red meat at least twice a day. A butcher, he states that he has no intention of quitting because he loves meat which is high in saturated fat.

Mr T.Y. has questions about this pending heart catheterization, though he had undergone one four years earlier. He is concerned about the risks of possible new percutaneous interventions, and fearful that his disease might be too advanced for any treatment. Mr. T.Y. is coping with his anxiety by reading the Bible and praying, talking to his family on the phone, and asking numerous questions of the staff about the procedure.

His nurse assessed him as eager and motivated to learn about the cardiac catheterization procedure, but only somewhat motivated to learn about the appropriate dietary management of his heart condition. He did ask questions about what would be healthy to eat, but when he was told what an optimal diet would be, he shook his head "No," indicating that a heart healthy diet as described was unacceptable.

A. Identify at least three high-priority learning needs (as evidenced by need for behavioral changes, not just by knowledge deficit) for Mr. T.Y.

_____

_____

_____

_____

_____

_____

B.   Using the four indicators (Table 4-2, p. 85) of physical, emotional, experiential and knowledge readiness, contrast Mr. T. Y.'s readiness to learn about the imminent procedure with his readiness to learn about healthy dietary changes.

_____

_____

_____

_____

_____

_____

_____

Links

The Paragon Learning Style Inventory (PLSI) is a self-administered survey that provides a very reliable indication of learning style and cognitive preference.

It uses the four Jungian dimensions (i.e., introversion/extroversion, intuition/sensation, thinking/feeling, and judging/perceiving) that are also used by the Myers-Briggs Type Indicator.

http://www.oswego.edu/plsi/

The Diablo Valley College Learning Style Survey was designed for college students to help them identify their learning styles. It also includes learning strategies that will help them study in a productive manner that matches their unique learning styles. The four learning styles in the DVC Survey are:

- Visual/Verbal
- Visual/Nonverbal
- Tactile/Kinesthetic
- Auditory/Verbal

http://www.metamath.com/lsweb/dvclearn.htm

CHAPTER 5

Developmental Stages
of the Learner

Critical Thinking

A. Chapter Summary: Write two or three sentences on what you understand to be the main idea(s) of Chapter 5:

_____

_____

_____

_____

_____

_____

_____

B. Debate: Do you agree or disagree with the following statement? Defend your position.

> . . . chronological age per se is not a good indicator of learning ability. At any given age, one finds a wide variation in the acquisition of abilities related to physical, cognitive and psychosocial maturation. (p. 120)

Small Group Discussion

Review the three adult learner categories described on pages 141–2 (goal-oriented, activity-oriented, and learning-oriented). Which of these best fits your reasons for pursuing further education?

Case Study

The Laurence G. Paquin School in North Baltimore, established in 1966, is reserved for childbearing adolescents (See Boyer-Patrick article in "Links" on p. 19). Pregnant female students from the city high schools are referred to Paquin School for the duration of their pregnancy. Pacquin School is always full. Pregnant teens from surrounding counties will move into a relative's home within the city limits in order to attend school there. Ninety-five percent of the student population is black, as is the principal, who fights vigorously to keep her students in school.

Besides a comprehensive academic program, other services include a Family Health Center on-site which offers prenatal care and counseling. If a teen delivers during the school year, she may finish that year at Paquin, bringing her baby with her to classes. This enables the new mother to participate in child care while attending classes herself. The father of the baby is also encouraged to attend pregnancy and child care classes.

L. J. is a typical student at Paquin School. She is unmarried and 15 years old. She moved to her grandmother's house in Northwest Baltimore from a nearby suburban community. This is her second pregnancy, the first ended in an abortion. The father of her baby is a first-year college student, and is staying involved with L. J. She hopes to return to her previous high school where she was on the track team, and eventually, to attend college herself.

After reading this case study, answer the questions that follow.

A. What different developmental tasks is this pregnant adolescent, L. J., facing at the same time?

_____

_____

_____

_____

_____

_____

_____

_____

B. What adaptations to the prepared childbirth classes offered by the school nurse might have to be made to accommodate the different developmental levels in the student population?

_____

_____

_____

_____

_____

_____

_____

C. Identify as many opportunities for health promotion as you can from the on-site childcare available for L. J. after she delivers her baby.

_____

_____

_____

_____

_____

_____

_____

Links

Boyer-Patrick, J. (1999). Use of counseling by pregnant or post-partum teens. Psychiatric Times, _16_(9), nd. Available at

http://psychiatrictimes.com/p990971.html

"The Children's Health Education Center" offers resources and programs for children, parents, teachers and caregivers to help keep kids healthy.

http://www.bluekids.org/teachers.asp

"Bandaids & Blackboards" provides a wide selection of health education topics written for children by a nurse educator.

http://www.lehman.cuny.edu/faculty/jfleitas/bandaides/joan.html

"Developmental Learning." This Webpage discusses learning as a constructive process. One's ability to learn develops over time as one matures. ("Teach Online" is an evolving site about pedagogy and techniques for fully online courses and for "hybrid" in person courses with an online component. The site is maintained by the Virtual University Design and Technology Group at Michigan State University.)

http://teachvu.vu.msu.edu/public/designers/what_is_learning/index.php?page_num=3

CHAPTER 6

Motivation, Compliance, and Health Behaviors of the Learner

Critical Thinking

A. Chapter Summary: Write two or three sentences on what you understand to be the main idea(s) of Chapter 6:

_____

_____

_____

_____

_____

_____

_____

B. Debate: Do you agree or disagree with the following statement? Defend your position.

> Learning occurs best when a state of moderate anxiety exists. In this optimum state for learning, one's ability to observe, focus attention, learn, and adapt is operative. (p. 165)

Small Group Discussion

Review the sub-roles of the nurse as educator, facilitator of change, contractor, organizer, and evaluator. (pp. 183–4) Which of these roles have you played the most in your career to date? Which have you used the least? How can you better incorporate all of the roles into your practice of health promotion?

Case Study

Read the following case study and answer the questions following. Also see the interactive case study and the learning case in "Links" below.

Mrs. A., a 67-year-old widow living alone, has been a diabetic since 1983. For at least 10 years prior to that she was symptomatic but undiagnosed, so systemic damage had probably started to occur. Many advances in diabetic treatment that make management more successful, and adherence to the recommended self-care regime easier for the patient, have been made since Mrs. A's diagnosis, such as the plate system for creating balanced meals, a 24-hour insulin pill and insulin pumps and pens, and glucose monitors that are lighter, quicker, and need very small blood samples. Mrs. A. still frequently skips her snacks, however, and does not monitor her blood glucose levels regularly. Oddly enough, she is most compliant when caring for her daughter's diabetic cat during her daughter's vacations. She has learned to test the cat's blood and give it insulin. Both she and the cat eat on time and ingest protein and snacks on a regular basis. Her blood sugars are within her norms and she feels better when she is caring for the cat.

A. What aspects of diabetes and its management make compliance with treatment plans more difficult?

_____

_____

_____

_____

_____

_____

_____

B. What factors may impede Mrs. A.'s self-care when she is alone? Why might caring for the cat change her behavior?

_____

_____

_____

_____

_____

_____

_____

Links

Interactive case study: "Promoting Behavior Change and Adherence: Options for Treatment." Patient & MD discuss diabetic management. The process is outlined in writing during the video. The viewer can click on sections of the outline to access a short "movie" disclosing background thoughts at that point in the discussion.

http://webcampus.drexelmed.edu/doccom/materials/movies/16%5FMedication/

The National Cancer Institute provides an extensive analysis of health promotion theory at this Web site. Part 1 discusses the "Foundations of Theory in Health Promotion and Health Behavior." Part 3 discusses "Putting Theory and Practice Together." Use the menu on the left to navigate to various sections of interest.

http://cancer.gov/cancerinformation/theory-at-a-glance

This problem-based learning case, "Don G. Smyth: Smoking Control," is designed to introduce the various concepts of smoking cessation counseling, behavioral diagnosis, targeted patient education and behavioral intervention. Materials and guides are provided for taking a smoking history, determining readiness to change and developing smoking cessation and health promotion interventions. A chapter from "How to help your patients stop smoking: A National Cancer Institute manual for physicians" is included (Phillips et al., 2000, University of Texas Medical Branch-Galveston and Leigh High Valley Hospital).

http://www.healcentral.org/content/6903/application/pdf/
    SMYTH_FINAL_GUIDE.pdf

CHAPTER 7

Literacy in the Adult Patient Population

Critical Thinking

A. Chapter Summary: Write two or three sentences on what you understand to be the main idea(s) of Chapter 7:

_____

_____

_____

_____

_____

_____

_____

B. Debate: Do you agree or disagree with the following statement? Defend your position.

> . . . complex and lengthy PEMs (printed educational materials) serve no useful teaching purpose if patients are unable to understand them or unwilling to read them. Literacy levels of patients compared with literacy demands of PEMs, whether in hospital or community-based settings, are an important factor in the rehabilitation and recidivism of patients. (p. 207)

Small Group Discussion

Read the five myths about illiteracy on page 200. Which one of these myths have you or your co-workers ever verbalized? How can this myth be challenged?

Case Study

After reading this case study, answer the questions following.

Mr. W., an 84-year-old, suffers from high blood pressure, atherosclerosis, and beginning glaucoma. He falls at a church function and is taken by ambulance to the emergency room. Unfortunately, his daughter, who usually accompanies him to his primary care clinic, is working. He refuses to have the staff "bother her at the job." Mr. W. cannot tell the emergency room nurse exactly what medications he is taking. He states that he takes a blue pill for his "high blood" in the morning, and two pink pills at dinner. He also says that he puts drops in his eyes every day. He nods his head when the emergency room staff tell him that his X-rays show no signs of a fracture, that he should consult his physician if a hematoma develops, elevate his left foot which is wrapped in an ace bandage, and apply ice packs for twenty-four hours. He signs the discharge form and receives printed instructions for care of a sprained ankle. An elderly friend who has followed the ambulance from church and stayed in the waiting room helps him into her car and drives him home.

A.   What are some signs in this scenario that Mr. W. suffers from health illiteracy?

_____

_____

_____

_____

_____

_____

_____

B.   How accurate or inaccurate might the claim be that Mr. W. has received appropriate discharge instructions?

_____

_____

_____

_____

_____

_____

_____

C. How could the emergency room staff have communicated better with Mr. W.?

_____

_____

_____

_____

_____

_____

_____

Links

"Clear Health Communication Initiative" is an extensive Web site devoted to improving health literacy. Understanding health information is everyone's right; improving clear health communication is everyone's responsibility. (Pfizer sponsored)

http://www.pfizerhealthliteracy.com/whatis.html

"Literacy and Health" is one complete issue of the Focus on Basics journal published by The National Center for the Study of Adult Learning and Literacy (NCSALL). This is a federally funded research and development center focused solely on adult learning.

http://www.ncsall.net/index.php?id=149

This Web page on health literacy offers a variety of adult activities to help develop positive health habits.

For each activity, visitors are provided with suggested materials to assist with the activity and the corresponding objectives. (Howard School of Public Health: Health Literacy Studies).

http://www.hsph.harvard.edu/healthliteracy/Health_activities.htm

CHAPTER 8

Gender, Socioeconomic, and Cultural Attributes of the Learner

Critical Thinking

A. Chapter Summary: Write two or three sentences on what you understand to be the main idea(s) of Chapter 8:

_____

_____

_____

_____

_____

_____

_____

B. Debate: Do you agree or disagree with the following statement? Defend your position.

> . . . individuals with literacy problems, poor educational backgrounds, and low academic achievement. . . . tend to think in concrete terms, are more focused on immediate needs, have a more external locus of control, and have decreased attention spans. They have difficulty problem solving and in analyzing and synthesizing large amounts of information. (p. 244)

Small Group Discussion

Read the definitions in the Nurse-Client Negotiations Model (pp. 249–50) of the popular, professional, and folk arenas. Does this model help explain the phenomenon of a nurse being asked by friends or family to diagnose or prescribe for a symptom?

Case Study

After reading this case study, answer the questions that follow.

A student nurse has been a member of a volunteer fire and rescue company for seven years. The student has decided to teach a health promotion class to this group. The ages of the 17 members range from 18 to 68; they are primarily male with four females. Since the U.S. Fire Administration listed heart attack as the number one cause of death for line-of-duty firefighters, the student chose to assess this group for cardiovascular disease risk factors. He identified stress, smoking, diet, and lack of exercise as risk factors. The working environment for the firefighters, as described by the student, is physically demanding. When on a call, they normally wear bulky gear, which can weigh 50 pounds or more. The fire-fighting environment is normally hot, humid, and stressful. In these conditions firefighters may need to run, crawl, chop with an axe, or drag heavy objects. The student chose to focus the health promotion class on the general risks of cardiovascular disease with an emphasis on the importance of exercise and physical fitness. His methods included PowerPoint lecture and role modeling using available exercise equipment.

A. Given the work environment and the gender mix of the learners, did the student choose an appropriate risk factor to emphasize?

_____

_____

_____

_____

_____

_____

_____

B. What additional learning activities might have been productive for this audience and topic?

_____

_____

_____

_____

_____

_____

_____

Links

Interactive case study: "Promoting Behavior Change and Adherence: Assessing the Patient's Situation. "A patient and a physician discuss diabetic management at this Web site. The process is outlined in writing during a brief video. The viewer can click on sections of the outline to access a short "movie" disclosing background thoughts at that point in the discussion.

http://webcampus.drexelmed.edu/doccom/materials/movies/16_Diet/

The Latino Health Institute is a community-based, professional organization that promotes the health of the community, its institutions, families, and individuals through effective interventions that are culturally competent and technologically appropriate.

www.lhi.org/

This site is the homepage of the Joint Center for Poverty Research, a national and interdisciplinary academic research center that seeks to advance our understanding of what it means to be poor in America. (Northwestern University and the University of Chicago)

www.jcpr.org/index.html

CHAPTER 9

Special Populations

Critical Thinking

A. Chapter Summary: Write two or three sentences on what you understand to be the main idea(s) of Chapter 9:

_____

_____

_____

_____

_____

_____

_____

B. Debate: In your opinion, is there any significant difference between Diehl's questions to determine the disabled person's readiness to learn (p. 282) and Lichtenthal's model for assessing readiness to learn as presented in Chapter 4 (pp. 84–93)? Defend your position.

_____

_____

_____

_____

_____

_____

_____

Small Group Discussion

Analyze an experience in your professional practice where you interacted with a person with hearing impairments or visual impairments. Use the guidelines on page 285 or page 286 to critique your interaction.

Case Study

After reading this case study, answer the questions that follow.

J.T. is a 48-year-old male African American with chronic undifferentiated schizophrenia. He is also obese and a smoker, with chronic hypertension, brittle diabetes with blood sugars normally 250–475 mg/dl, and has a history of alcohol abuse. He is often admitted, stabilized, discharged and readmitted to a state-run hospital for the mentally ill. He has delusions and hallucinations and reports being a space traveler who likes to blow up buildings. J.T. is 6′6″ tall, weighs 267 lbs and intentionally intimidates peers and staff. When not in the hospital, J.T. lives in group home settings that frequently change, or with an elderly grandmother who has difficulty mana verbal communication skill often seen with schizophrenic patients. He is beginning to suffer from severe headaches and visual problems. He has voiced fears of losing body parts related to poor diabetic management, but at times is confused and delusional and sees himself as invincible.

A.   Evaluate this client's readiness to learn. What are positive and negative factors that might affect the chances of learning success?

_____

_____

_____

_____

_____

_____

_____

After a first teaching session about nutrition and insulin therapy, J.T. was able to verbalize an understanding of his salt and sugar restrictions, and was able to identify correctly the areas of his body where insulin should be given. However, his parting comment was, "I will take the shot but if you try and take my snacks or cookies away, I will blow up your house!"

B. How should this client's schizophrenia influence the planning for future health education sessions?

_____

_____

_____

_____

_____

_____

_____

Links

The National Center on Physical Activity and Disabilities (NCPAD) offers many resources for adapted services. This site provides numerous links to specific disabilities and chronic health conditions that impact activity choices.

http://www.ncpad.org/disability/

"Family Caregivers Online" is a Web site that offers user-friendly educational modules and other information resources to caregivers of the elderly and chronically ill.

http://www.familycaregiversonline.com/index.html

Phelan, M., Stradins, L., and Morrison, S. (2001). Physical health of people with severe mental illness (Editorial). _British Medical Journal_, 322, 443–44.

http://bmj.bmjjournals.com/cgi/content/full/322/7284/443

CHAPTER 10

Behavioral Objectives

Critical Thinking

A. Chapter Summary: Write two or three sentences on what you understand to be the main idea(s) of Chapter 10:

_____

_____

_____

_____

_____

_____

_____

B. Debate: Do you agree or disagree with the following statement? Defend your position.

> The writing of objectives is not merely a mechanical task but a synthesizing process . . . the setting of objectives and goals is considered by many to be the initial, most important consideration in the educational process." (pp. 323–4)

Small Group Discussion

Review the "Common Mistakes when Writing Objectives" and Table 10-3 on pp. 326–7. Which of these mistakes have you made the most frequently when writing objectives? (If you have not written educational objectives, review your experience writing objectives for nursing care plans.) How can you improve your setting of goals and objectives?

Case Study

After reading this case study, answer the questions that follow.

A nurse who works in the Neonatal Intensive Care Unit (NICU) has been assigned to develop a teaching plan for the parents of premature babies who are nearly ready for discharge. The parents are predominantly white and Hispanic, with ages ranging from 15 to 47. The infants may have any number of physical needs upon discharge including special feeding instructions, apnea monitors, temperature instability, colostomy care, and oxygen supplementation, among others. The parents will be anxious, tired, disoriented, and possibly in pain (post-caesarean section mothers). The NICU can be an intimidating and distracting place for learning, with monitor noise, dim or bright lighting, multiple staff members performing multiple procedures, and the potential for life-threatening crises.

Before writing learning objectives, the nurse establishes three priority educational needs (diagnoses): (a) risk for abnormal body temperature fluctuations, (b) risk for ineffective breathing patterns, and (c) altered nutrition: less than body requirements.

She has difficulty formulating learning objectives at this point.

A. What is the problem with the focus of this needs list? Rewrite the needs list to better reflect the purpose of the teaching plan.

_____

_____

_____

_____

_____

_____

After reframing her prioritized educational needs (diagnoses), the nurse writes the following learning objective, "Parents will verbalize correct feeding procedures for breast and bottle feedings and demonstrate competency in feeding infant in one or both ways that are chosen to feed infant."

B. What are the strong and weak points of this learning objective? Rewrite the learning objective addressing the weak areas.

_____

_____

_____

_____

_____

_____

_____

Links

"I.O.W.A.: Instructional Objectives Writing Assistant." This interactive Web site is a research project that is designed to help instructors write better learning objectives. (School of Civil and Environmental Engineering, Georgia Institute of Technology)

http://epitome.ce.gatech.edu/iowa/index.html

"Instructional Objectives." This Web page discusses behavioral, cognitive and constructivist learning objectives. Instructional objectives define target-learning goals for an educational experience. A self-test is included. ("Teach Online" is maintained by the Virtual University Design and Technology Group at Michigan State University.)

http://teachvu.vu.msu.edu/public/designers/teaching_and_learning/index. php?page_num=7

"A Quick Guide to Writing Learning Objectives" provides an outline and templates for writing learning objectives according to the tasks, the conditions, and the standards desired. A link to Bloom's taxonomy is provided.

http://www.nwlink.com/~donclark/hrd/templates/templates.html#LO

CHAPTER 11

Instructional Methods

Critical Thinking

A. Chapter Summary: Write two or three sentences on what you understand to be the main idea(s) of Chapter 11:

_____

_____

_____

_____

_____

_____

_____

B. Debate: Do you agree or disagree with the following statement? Defend your position.

> The use of different types of technology assists the teacher in helping learners meet their individual needs and styles of learning. Technology has the potential for making the teaching-learning process more convenient, accessible, and stimulating. (p. 382)

Small Group Discussion

Choose one of the case studies in chapters 4–7 of the Student Lecture Companion that present scenarios of individual patients. What traditional method of instruction (pp. 357–66) would you choose for your patient, and why? Which non-traditional method (pp. 366–77), and why?

Case Study

After reading this case study, answer the questions that follow.

Mrs. G.'s elderly father has had a massive stroke with life-limiting consequences. It has been decided that hospice care will be initiated within the acute care facility, since his life expectancy is measured in days, and he is no longer conscious. The hospice intake nurse meets with the immediate family several times in the first 48 hours, to explain the options and assist in decision-making choices. Other team members (either participating in the meetings or on-call) include the hospital palliative care team, the nursing staff, the physician, the chaplain, and the social worker. Meetings are held in a private area away from the patient's room, but with on-call communication available.

This hospital has planned a series of topics that need to be presented in such a situation. The first meeting covers prognosis, code status, and treatment options. The second meeting discusses nutrition and hydration and treatment of concurrent illnesses (if present). The third meeting discusses palliative care and hospice and the scope of available resources. The fourth meeting introduces the concept of de-escalating care, initiation of comfort measures, and involvement of family and friends. Optional information will include spiritual care, the grieving process, and stress management.

There are opportunities for questions at each session. Meetings will not always be separate or proceed in the same order. Multiple sessions of the same content may be needed before all family members can be reached. Any member of the team is trained to reinforce any content. Written material is available for all content, but is only given out after a face-to-face meeting. Readiness to learn must be evaluated on a continual basis. Due to the highly stressful nature of the content, timing of education may need to be adjusted differently for different family members.

A.   What methodology has this program chosen to implement? Is it appropriate to the situation?

_____

_____

_____

_____

_____

_____

_____

B. Compare and contrast the aspects of flexibility and structure in this program. What is the rationale for considering each aspect in planning? How have these considerations influenced methodology choices?

_____

_____

_____

_____

_____

_____

_____

Links

This link discusses teaching and learning styles. Teacher-centered styles are explained in detail. (The "Teach Online" site is maintained by the Virtual University Design and Technology Group at Michigan State University)

http://teachvu.vu.msu.edu/public/designers/teaching_and_learning/

"How do I choose a teaching method?" Learn more about when to use the following methods and the advantages and disadvantages of each: teacher centered, interactive, individualized, and experiential. From the "Curriculum Development Resources Web site of Fanshawe College, Ontario, Canada.

http://gs.fanshawec.on.ca/cdr/how_do_i_choose_a_teaching_metho.htm

"Lecture Approach" presents creative ways to use lecture as a teaching methodology and suggestions to enhance attention, participation and learning. (Indiana State University, "Teaching Tips Archives")

http://www.indstate.edu/cirt/pd/tips/lecture.htm

CHAPTER 12

Instructional Materials

Critical Thinking

A. Chapter Summary: Write two or three sentences on what you understand to be the main idea(s) of Chapter 12:

_____

_____

_____

_____

_____

_____

_____

B. Debate: Review the section on commercially-prepared teaching materials on pp. 394–5. Take a stand on the issue of using free patient education materials provided by drug or formula manufacturers. Defend your position.

Small Group Discussion

Critique your workplace or clinical setting for its use of printed educational materials. Are they the only type available? Are they used appropriately? What other types of materials might be beneficial to the patients in your work setting?

Case Study

After reading this case study, answer the questions that follow.

Due to the increased volume of patients, a 75-minute pre-operative class has been planned for patients scheduled for knee replacement surgery. This will replace individual pre-operative teaching, and will take place the evening before admission for surgery at the Joint Replacement Center. Past experience with individuals leads the nurse educator to expect motivated, attentive, moderately anxious participants. The target audience will be primarily over 60 years old, have regular access to health care, and no other health problems severe enough to rule out the surgery. Occasionally, obesity and diabetes join the primary diagnosis of arthritis. The class will consist of a PowerPoint lecture created by the nurse on the topics of pre-operative preparation, pain control, infection, anticoagulation therapy, incentive spirometry, physical therapy, dietary changes for weight reduction, and discharge planning. In addition, an invited speaker who has undergone the procedure will discuss the recovery period. Models of the knee joint will be used to demonstrate lecture points. A PCA pump will be available for simulated use. Booklets from the manufacturers of anticoagulants will be given out. Outcomes of class attendance are expected to be effective use of pain control measures, participation in physical therapy exercises and respiratory toilet, performance of DVT prevention exercises, and freedom from operative site infection at follow-up.

A. Critique the PowerPoint lecture for length and completeness of content.

_____

_____

_____

_____

_____

_____

_____

B. What additional teaching materials (beyond the knee model, the booklets, and the PCA pump) would add to the quality of this course?

_____

_____

_____

_____

_____

_____

_____

Links

"How to Create and Assess Print Materials" discusses reading skills, creating materials, and assessing materials for both printed materials and Web sites. (Harvard School of Public Health: Health Literacy Studies)

http://www.hsph.harvard.edu/healthliteracy/materials.html

"Learning Objects" are digital resources that are used to support learning. This Web site contains multiple links to sample online learning objects. ("Teach Online" is an evolving site about pedagogy and techniques for fully online courses and for "hybrid" in-person courses with an online component. The site is maintained by the Virtual University Design and Technology Group at Michigan State University.)

http://teachvu.vu.msu.edu/public/designers/learning_elements/
  index.php?page_num=8

"A Lifespan Approach to Health Education: An Evaluation Instrument for Instructional Materials" provides a means for assessing the degree to which textbooks and instructional materials in health education contain accurate and necessary information about aging across the lifespan. (National Academy for Teaching and Learning about Aging)

http://www.cps.unt.edu/natla/rsrc/lifespan_health_ed.pdf

The "Patient Education Materials" Web site outlines resources the nurse can call upon to help develop written materials for patients and their families, and provides some basic tips for effective patient teaching. (University of Utah Health Sciences Center)

http://uuhsc.utah.edu/pated/

CHAPTER 13

Technology in Education

Critical Thinking

A. Chapter Summary: Write two or three sentences on what you understand to be the main idea(s) of Chapter 13:

_____

_____

_____

_____

_____

_____

_____

B. Debate: Do you agree or disagree with the following statement? Defend your position.

When information is widely available, the teacher is no longer the person who holds all the answers or the individual who is solely responsible for imparting knowledge. Therefore, educators in the Information Age are becoming facilitators of learning rather than providers of information . . . (p. 432)

Small Group Discussion

Review Table 13-3, "Criteria for evaluating health-related Web sites" (p. 441). How would these criteria help you in evaluating sources for your own research?

Case Study

After reading this case study, answer the questions and complete the exercise that follows.

Mrs. F. is a 78-year-old widow with a high-school education. Her medical problems include hypertension, hypercholesterolemia, and a history of transient ischemic attacks. She has had lens implants for bilateral cataracts. Her children have just purchased a computer for Mrs. F. and helped her learn how to access the Internet. She enjoys e-mailing distant family and friends, and shopping online. At her next outpatient visit, she asks about the benefits of eating organic foods to prevent cancer and the use of herbal supplements to stimulate her immune system for fighting influenza.

A. What questio ns would you ask Mrs. F. about her sources of health information?

_____

_____

_____

_____

_____

_____

_____

You refer Mrs. F. to the URL www.health.gov/scipich/. "SciPICH: Science Panel on Interactive Communication and Health" is a Web site designed to help inform consumers on how to navigate the new technologies and health resources on the Web in order to locate the best information resources. Consumers can take the exercises on this site and learn how to recognize quality information. (Sponsored by the Office of Disease Prevention and Health Promotion, U.S. Dept. of Health and Human Services.)

B. Access "SciPICH". Locate and list below several specific tips and exercises that would be appropriate for Mrs. F.'s age and health history.

_____

_____

_____

_____

_____

_____

Links

"Featured Approaches" for online learning presents several methods for enriching online classes. ("Teach Online" is an evolving site about pedagogy and techniques for fully online courses and for "hybrid" in-person courses with an online component. The site is maintained by the Virtual University Design and Technology Group at Michigan State University.)

http://teachvu.vu.msu.edu/public/designers/featured_approaches/

"The Health Education Assets Library" provides free, high-quality digital materials for health sciences education. Hosting institutions include the Universities of Utah and Oklahoma, and UCLA. This project is grant-funded by the National Sciences Foundation and the National Library of Medicine.

http://www.healcentral.org/

"Guidelines for Medical and Health Information Sites on the Internet". The site follows principles which govern all aspects of AMA Web sites: Content, advertising and sponsorship, Website privacy and confidentiality, and E-Commerce. (American Medical Association)

http://www.ama-assn.org/ama/pub/category/1905.html

CHAPTER 14

Instructional Settings

Critical Thinking

A. Chapter Summary: Write two or three sentences on what you understand to be the main idea(s) of Chapter 14:

_____

_____

_____

_____

_____

_____

_____

B. Debate: Review the classification of instructional settings (pp. 467–9). Do you agree or disagree with the text's emphasis on the "primary function of an organization" as a defining element in planning patient education encounters? Defend your position.

Small Group Discussion

What are the situational constraints on optimal patient education at your health care facility? Are they primarily organizational, resource-related or patient-related factors?

Case Study

Review the scenario on pages 478–9. Two different clients are admitted to a same-day surgery unit. One is a housewife with limited English proficiency, and the other is a schoolteacher. After reading this scenario, answer the questions that follow.

A. What are the organizational, resource, and patient-related factors that would affect patient education in this scenario?

_____

_____

_____

_____

_____

_____

_____

B. Critique the adaptations that the outpatient surgery unit has chosen to address the above factors. What improvements might you suggest?

_____

_____

_____

_____

_____

_____

C. Are the adaptations in place appropriate for both patients as described in the scenario?

_____

_____

_____

_____

_____

_____

_____

Links

Interactive case study: "Informed Decision-making: the Importance of Giving Options to the Patient." A patient and doctor discuss starting insulin. The process is outlined during the video. The viewer can click on sections of the outline to access a short "movie" disclosing either the patient or the doctor's thoughts at that point in the discussion.

http://webcampus.drexelmed.edu/doccom/materials/movies/
    17%5FGivingOptions

"Collaborative/Cooperative Learning Environments" presents creative ways to incorporate community, teamwork, and small groups to enhance attention, participation and learning. (Indiana State University, "Teaching Tips Archives")

http://www.indstate.edu/cirt/pd/tips/collaborative.htm

Evaluation in Healthcare Education

Critical Thinking

A. Chapter Summary: Write two or three sentences on what you understand to be the main idea(s) of Chapter 15:

_____

_____

_____

_____

_____

_____

_____

B. Debate: Do you agree or disagree with the following statement? Defend your position.

Because you may conduct an evaluation at the end of your program, do not assume that you should plan it at this point in time. Evaluation as an afterthought is, at best, a poor idea, and, at worst, a dangerous one. (p. 494)

Small Group Discussion

Review "Process (Formative) Evaluation" (pp. 496–8). What adjustments have you made in an educational activity as soon as they were needed? What led you to make those adjustments? How successful were they?

Case Study

After reading this research abstract, answer the questions that follow.

Bowman, A. and Epp, D. (2005). Rural diabetes education: does it make a difference? *Canadian Journal of Nursing Research*, 37(1), 34–53.

This cross-sectional study using a mailed survey evaluated outcomes of diabetes education, care, and support provided at two clinics in rural Manitoba, Canada. Seventy-eight respondents with type 2 diabetes, including 51 rural clinic attenders and 27 non-attenders (mean age = 68.5), were compared regarding demographic characteristics; diabetes education and knowledge; diabetes self-management efficacy, attitudes, and behaviors; quality of life; satisfaction with care; and health-care utilization. Attenders had more diabetes education ($P < .001$), higher self-management efficacy scores ($P < .051$), and greater satisfaction with diabetes care ($P < .001$) than non-attenders, but more education did not translate into greater diabetes-related knowledge, attitudes, or behaviors. While clinic attendance and supportive interaction with health professionals and peers may help equip people with type 2 diabetes with the confidence and alternative strategies to handle diabetes-related health problems, a more standard approach to diabetes education and care could improve the achievement of desired outcomes. (School of Health Studies, Brandon University, Manitoba, Canada.)

A. What is the result of the comparison of patient outcomes in the attenders versus the non-attenders at the two clinics?

_____

_____

_____

_____

_____

_____

_____

B. The authors conclude that certain program changes might improve the situation. Is this justified based on the results as reported in the abstract?

_____

_____

_____

_____

_____

_____

_____

Links

This is an extensive evaluation tool to document the competency of the health education teacher, not the course, class or instructional event.

http://www.isbe.state.il.us/profprep/CASCDvr/Wd97/27280_healtheduc.doc

Martins, E. N. and Morse, L. S. (2005). Evaluation of internet websites about retinopathy of prematurity patient education. _British Journal of Ophthalmology, 89_(5), 565–8.

http://bjo.bmjjournals.com/cgi/content/full/89/5/565

Gerber, B. S., Brodsky, I. G., Lawless, K. A., Smolin, L. I., Arozullah, A. M., Smith, E. V., Berbaum, M. L., Heckerling, P. S., and Eiser, A. R. (2005). Implementation and evaluation of a low-literacy diabetes education computer multimedia application. _Diabetes Care, 28_(7), 1574–80.

http://care.diabetesjournals.org/cgi/content/full/28/7/1574

Notes

Chapter 1

Overview of Education in Health
Care

Historical Foundations of the Nurse's Role as Teacher

- Health education has long been considered a function of standard care given by the nurse.
- Patient teaching is recognized as an independent nursing function.
- Nursing practice has expanded to include education in the broad concepts of health and illness.

Historical Foundations (cont'd)

- Standards and Mandates for Patient Education by Professional Organizations and Agencies:
1. NLNE (NLN)
   - first observed health teaching as an important function within the scope of nursing practice
   - Responsible for identifying course content for curriculum on principles of teaching and learning

Historical Foundations (cont'd)

2. ANA
   - Responsible for establishing standards and qualifications for practice, including patient teaching
3. ICN
   - Endorses health education as an essential component of nursing care delivery

Historical Foundations (cont'd)

4. State Nurse Practice Acts
   - Universally include teaching within the scope of nursing practice
5. JCAHO
   - Accreditation mandates require evidence of patient education to improve outcomes
6. AHA
   - *Patient's Bill of Rights* ensures that clients receive complete and current information

Historical Foundations (cont'd)

7. PEW Health Professions Commission
   - Set forth health profession competencies for the 21st century
   - Provides recommendations pertaining to importance of patient education

Trends Impacting on Health Care

- Social, economic, and political forces impacting on nurse's role in teaching:
  - Federal initiatives outlined in *Healthy People 2010*
  - Growth of managed care
  - Increased attention to health and well-being of everyone in society
  - Cost containment measures to control
  - Healthcare expenses
  - Advanced technology increasing complexity of care and treatment

Trends (cont'd)

- Consumers demanding more knowledge and skills for self-care
- Demographic trends influencing type and amount of health care needed
- Increased recognition of the need for prevention and promotion efforts

Purpose, Goal, and Benefits of Patient Education

- Purpose: to increase the competence and confidence of patients to manage their own self-care
- Goal: to increase self-care responsibility of clients and to improve the quality of care delivered by nurses

Purpose, Goal, and Benefits (cont'd)

- Benefits of education to patients:
  - Increase consumer satisfaction
  - Improve quality of life
  - Ensure continuity of care
  - Reduce incidence of illness complications
  - Increase compliance with treatment
  - Decrease anxiety
  - Maximize independence

ASSURE Model

A useful paradigm to assist nurses to organize and carry out the education process.

Analyze the learner

State objectives

Select teaching methods and tools

Use teaching methods and tools

Require learner performance

Evaluate as necessary the teaching and revise

Role of the Nurse as Teacher

- Nurses act in the role of teacher for patients and their family members, nursing students

Role of Nurse as Teacher (cont'd)

- Nurses function in the role of teachers as:
  - The givers of information
  - The facilitators of learning
  - The coordinators of teaching
  - The advocates of the client
- The nurse's role in educating others stems from the philosophy that stresses mutual partnership and active participation by the nurse and patient in the teaching and learning process.

Barriers to Teaching

- *Barriers* to teaching are those factors interfering with the nurse's ability to optimally deliver educational services.
- Major barriers include:
  - Lack of time to teach due to patient shortened lengths of hospital stays, and the nature of nurse/ patient contact in various settings
  - Inconsistent coordination and inadequate documentation negatively impacts on the quality and quantity of teaching efforts
  - Inadequate preparation of nurses in the principles of teaching and learning to assume the role of teacher with confidence and competence

Barriers to Education (cont'd)

- Low priority status and limited financial resources given to teaching when other task-oriented responsibilities take precedence
- Environment not conducive to carrying out patient education
- Lack of 3rd party reimbursement to support education efforts.
- Lack of commitment to the concept of the "utility" of patient education.

Obstacles to Learning

- *Obstacles* to learning are those factors that negatively impact on the learner's ability to attend to and process information.
- Major obstacles include:
  - Limited time due to rapid discharge from care stress of acute and chronic illness, anxiety, sensory deficits, and low literacy
  - Lack of privacy or social isolation of health-care environment

Obstacles (cont'd)

  - Situational and personal variations in readiness to learn, motivation and compliance, and learning styles
  - Extent of behavioral changes (in number and complexity) required
  - Lack of support and positive reinforcement from providers and/or significant others

Obstacles (cont'd)

  - Psychological factors of denial of learning needs, resentment of authority, and locus of control
  - Inconvenience, complexity, inaccessibility, and fragmentation of the health-care system

Information in Literature on Patient and Staff Education

- Most non-research-based literature focuses on "how to do" patient teaching
- More information exists on the psychological advantages rather than the physiological outcomes of patient education
- More attention is given to the needs of learners who have acute, short-term problems than those who have chronic, long-term conditions

Information in Literature (cont'd)

- More research needed on the availability, benefits, and effectiveness of innovative teaching methods and tools
- Need further investigation on the cost-effectiveness of education efforts
- Future research must address:
  - Measurement of behavioral outcomes
  - Effects of educational interventions
  - Influence of intervening variables
  - Theoretical basis for education in practice

Questions To Be Asked

- The following questions can be asked about the principles of teaching and learning:
- How can the health-care team work more effectively together to coordinate educational efforts?
- What are the ethical, legal, and economic, issues involved in patient?
- How can learning theories be applied to change the behaviors of learners?
- What assessment methods can be used to determine learning needs, readiness to learn, and learning styles?

Notes

Questions (cont'd)

- How can teaching be tailored to meet the needs of specific clientele?
- What learning attributes positively and negatively affect an individual's ability and willingness to learn?
- What factors influence motivation and compliance to achieve desired outcomes?
- Which elements need to be taken into account when developing teaching plans?
- What teaching methods and tools are available to support patient education?

Questions (cont'd)

- Under what conditions should certain teaching methods and tools be used?
- What are the common mistakes made when teaching patients and their families?
- How are teaching and learning best evaluated?

What other questions might you ask?

Chapter 2: Ethical, Legal, and Economic Foundations of the Educational Process

Notes

Chapter 2

Ethical, Legal, and Economic Foundations
of the Educational Process

Evolution of Ethical/Legal Principles in Health Care

1. Natural Law
2. Charitable Immunity
3. Cardozo Decision of 1914
   A. Informed consent
   B. Right to self-determination

Cardozo Decision

A. Informed Consent: the right to full disclosure; the right to make one's own decisions
B. Right to self-determination: the right to protect one's own body and to determine how it shall be treated

---

Government Regulations & Professional Standards

1. National Commission for the Protection of Human Subjects of Biomedical and Behavioral Research
2. President's Commission for the Study of Ethical Problems in Medicine and Biomedical and Behavioral Research
3. American Nurses Association's *Code for Nurses with Interpretative Statements*
4. American Hospital Association's *Patient's Bill of Rights*

Application of Ethical Principles

1. Autonomy
2. Veracity
3. Nonmalfeasance
   A. Negligence
   B. Malpractice
   C. Duty
4. Confidentiality
5. Beneficence
6. Justice

Definition of Ethical Principles

1. **Autonomy:** the right of a client to self-determination
2. **Veracity:** truth telling; the honesty by a professional in providing full disclosure to a client of the risks and benefits of any invasive medical procedure

Definition of Ethical Principles (cont'd)

1. **Nonmalfeasance:** the principle of doing no harm

   A. **Negligence:** the doing or nondoing of an act, persuant to a duty, that a reasonable person in the same circumstances would or would not do, with these actions or non-actions leading to injury of another person or his/her property.

Definition of Ethical Principles (cont'd)

   B. **Malpractice:** refers to a limited class of negligent activities that fall within the scope of performance by those pursuing a particular profession involving highly skilled and technical services.

Definition of Ethical Principles (cont'd)

   C. **Duty:** a standard of behavior; a behavioral expectation relevant to one's personal or professional status in life.

Notes

Definition of Ethical Principles (cont'd)

4. **Confidentiality:** a binding social contract or covenant to protect another's privacy; a professional obligation to respect privileged information between health professional and client.

5. **Beneficence:** The principle of doing good; of acting in the best interest of a client through adherence to professional performance standards and procedural protocols.

Definition of Ethical Principles (cont'd)

6. **Justice:** Equal distribution of goods, services, benefits, and burdens regardless of client diagnosis, culture, national origin, religious orientation, sexual preference and the like.

Ethical/Legal Foundations of Patient Education

A. **Mandates:**

1. Joint Commission on Accreditation of Health-Care Organizations
2. State Regulations
3. Federal Regulations
4. Nurse Practice Acts

Notes

Ethical/Legal Foundations of Patient Education (cont'd)

B. Documentation:

1. **Third Party Reimbursement:** revenue generated from insurance companies, from federally funded Medicare and Medicaid programs, or from patient's personal finances ("private pay")

2. **"Respondeat Superior":** refers to the "Master-Servant" rule: The employer may be held liable for the negligence or other unlawful acts of the employee during the performance of his or her job-related responsibilities.

Economic Factors Influencing Patient Education

A. Financial Terminology
  1. Direct Costs
    a. Fixed
    b. Variable
  2. Indirect Costs

Economic Factors Influencing Patient Education (cont'd)

1. **Direct Costs:** those that are tangible and predictable such as rent, food, heating, etc.

   a. **Fixed Costs:** those that are stable and ongoing, such as salaries, mortgage, utilities, durable equipment, etc.

   b. **Variable Costs:** those related to fluctuation in volume, program attendance, occupancy rates, etc.

Economic Factors Influencing Patient Education (cont'd)

2. **Indirect Costs:** those that may be fixed but not necessarily directly related to a particular activity, such as expenses of heating, lighting, housekeeping, maintenance, etc.

Economic Factors Influencing Patient Education (cont'd)

B. Cost Factors:
   1. Cost Savings
   2. Cost Benefit
   3. Cost Recovery

Economic Factors Influencing Patient Education (cont'd)

1. **Cost Savings:** money realized through decreased use of costly services, shortened lengths of stay, or fewer complications resulting from preventive services or patient education.

Economic Factors Influencing Patient Education (cont'd)

2. **Cost Benefit:** occurs when the institution realizes an economic gain resulting from the educational program, such as a drop in re-admission rates.

Economic Factors Influencing Patient Education (cont'd)

3. **Cost Recovery:** occurs when revenues generated are equal to or greater than expenditures.

Economic Factors Influencing Patient Education (cont'd)

C. Program Planning: Relationships and Outcomes
   1. Cost-Effectiveness Analysis
   2. Cost-Benefit Analysis

Program Planning

- Relationship of Costs & Outcomes
  1. **Cost-Effectiveness Analysis:** refers to determining the economic value of an educational offering by making a comparison between two or more programs, based on reliable measures of positive changes in the behaviors of participants as well as evidence of maintenance of these behaviors, when a real monetary value cannot be assigned to the achievement of program outcomes.

Program Planning (cont'd)

  2. **Cost-Benefit Analysis:** the relationship (ratio) between actual program costs and actual program benefits, as measured in monetary terms, to determine if revenue generation was realized.

Summary

- Patient teaching is an ethical and legal responsibility of the nurse
- Patient teaching protects the human rights of self-determination and informed consent
- The role of the nurse as teacher is addressed in NPAs of each state

Notes

Chapter 3

Learning Theory and Nursing
Practice

Learning

- Learning: a relatively permanent change in mental processing, emotional functioning, and behavior as a result of experience
- Learning Theory: a coherent framework and set of integrated constructs and principles directed toward describing, explaining, and predicting learning

---

Contribution of Learning Theories

- Provides information and techniques to guide teaching and learning
- Can be employed singly or in combination
- Can be applied in a variety of settings as well as for personal growth and interpersonal relations

---

Guiding Questions

- How do the environment and the internal dynamics of the individual influence learning?
- Is the learner viewed as passive or active?
- What is the educator's task?
- What motivates individuals to learn?
- What encourages transfer of learning?

Behaviorist Theory

- Concepts: stimulus conditions, reinforcement, response, drive
- To change behavior, change the stimulus conditions in the environment and the reinforcement after a response

Behaviorist Dynamics

- Motivation: drives to be reduced, incentives
- Educator: active role; manipulates environmental stimuli and reinforcements to direct change
- Transfer: practice and provide similarity in stimulus conditions and responses with new situation

Respondent Conditioning

- Learning occurs as the organism responds to stimulus conditions and forms associations
- A neutral stimulus is paired with an unconditioned stimulus-unconditioned response connection until the neutral stimulus becomes a conditioned stimulus that elicits the conditioned response

Operant Conditioning

- Learning occurs as the organism responds to stimuli in the environment and is reinforced for making a particular response
- A reinforcer applied after a response strengthens the probability that the response will be performed again under similar conditions

Changing Behavior Using Operant Conditioning

- To increase behavior
  - Positive reinforcement
  - Negative reinforcement (escape or avoidance conditioning)
- To decrease behavior
  - Nonreinforcement
  - Punishment

Notes

Notes

Cognitive Theory

- Concepts: cognition, gestalt, perception, developmental stage, information-processing, memory, social constructivism, social cognition, attributions
- To change behavior, work with the developmental stage and change cognitions, goals, expectations, equilibrium, and ways of processing information

Cognitive Dynamics

- Motivation: goals, expectations, disequilibrium, cultural and group values
- Educator: organize experiences and make them meaningful; encourage insight and reorganization within learner
- Transfer: focus on internal processes and provide common patterns with new situation

Gestalt Perspective

- Perception and the patterning of stimuli (gestalt) are the keys to learning, with each learner perceiving, interpreting, and reorganizing experiences in her/his own way
- Learning occurs through the reorganization of elements to form new insights and understanding

Information-Processing Perspective

- The way individuals perceive, process, store, and retrieve information from experiences determines how learning occurs and what is learned
- Organizing information and making it meaningful aids the attention and storage process; learning occurs through guidance, feedback, assessing and correcting errors

Cognitive Development Perspective

- Learning depends on the stage of cognitive functioning, with qualitative, sequential changes in perception, language, and thought occurring as children and adults interact with the environment
- Recognize the developmental stage and provide appropriate experiences to encourage discovery

Social Constructivist Perspective

- Learning is heavily influenced by the culture and occurs as a social process in interaction with others
- A person's knowledge may not necessarily reflect reality, but through collaboration and negotiation, new understanding is acquired

Social Cognition Perspective

- An individual's perceptions, beliefs, and social judgments are strongly affected by social interaction, communication, groups, and the social situation
- Individuals formulate causal explanations to account for behavior that have significant consequences for their attitudes and actions (attribution theory)

Social Learning Theory

- Concepts: role modeling, vicarious reinforcement, self-system, self-regulation
- To change behavior, utilize effective role models who are perceived to be rewarded, and work with the social situation and the learner's internal self-regulating mechanisms

Social Learning Dynamics

- Motivation: compelling role models perceived to be rewarded, self-system regulating behavior, self-efficacy
- Educator: model behavior and demonstrate benefits; encourage active learner to regulate and reproduce behavior
- Transfer: similarity of setting, feedback, self-efficacy, social influences

Psychodynamic Theory

- Concepts: stage of personality development, conscious and unconscious motivations, ego-strength, emotional conflicts, defense mechanisms
- To change behavior, work to make unconscious motivations conscious, build ego-strength, and resolve emotional conflicts

Psychodynamic Dynamics

- Motivation: libido, life force, death wish, pleasure principle, reality principle, conscious and unconscious conflicts, developmental stage, defenses
- Educator: reflective interpreter; listen and pose questions to stimulate insights
- Transfer: remove barriers such as resistance, transference reactions, emotional conflicts

Humanistic Theory

- Learning occurs on the basis of a person's motivation, derived from needs, the desire to grow in positive ways, self-concept, and subjective feelings
- Learning is facilitated by caring facilitators and a nurturing environment that encourage spontaneity, creativity, emotional expression, and positive choices

Notes

Humanist Dynamics

- Motivation: needs, desire to grow, self-concept
- Educator: act as facilitator who respects learner's uniqueness and provides freedom to feel, express, and grow creatively
- Transfer: positive or negative feelings and choices as well as freedom to learn promote or inhibit transfer

Environmental Influences (External)

- Stimulus conditions and configuration of elements
- Social and cultural influences
- Role models, experts, and guides
- Reinforcements
- Feedback

Learner Influences (Internal)

- Developmental stage
- Habits
- Perception
- Thoughts and reasoning
- Schema
- Ways of processing information
- Memory storage

Learner Influences (Internal) (cont'd)

- Conscious and unconscious motivation
- Self-regulation
- Subjective feelings
- Self-concept
- Expectations
- Goals
- Needs

How to Promote Change

- Relate to what learner knows and is familiar
- Keep experiences simple, organized and meaningful
- Motivate learner (deprivation, goals, disequilibrium, needs, tension)
- May need incentives and rewards, but not always

How to Promote Change (cont'd)

- Experiences must be at appropriate developmental level
- Make learning pleasurable not painful
- Demonstrate by guidance and attractive role models

Notes

How to Make Learning Relatively Permanent

- Relate experiences to learner
- Reinforce behavior
- Rehearse and practice in variety of settings
- Have learner perform and give constructive feedback
- Make sure interference does not occur before, during, or after learning

How to Make Learning Relatively Permanent (cont'd)

- Promote transfer
- Have learner mediate and act on experience in some way (visualize, memory devices, discuss, talk, discuss, write, motor movement)

Questions to Consider

- In what ways do the learning theories differ?
- In what ways are they similar?
- How can the learning theories be used in combination to change behavior and enhance learning?
- Why are some theories more effective with certain individuals than with others?

Notes

_____
_____
_____
_____
_____
_____
_____
_____
_____
_____
_____
_____
_____
_____
_____
_____
_____
_____
_____
_____
_____
_____
_____
_____
_____
_____
_____
_____
_____
_____
_____
_____
_____
_____
_____
_____
_____
_____

Chapter 4

Determinants of Learning

Educator's Role in Learning

- The educator plays a crucial role in the learning process by:
- assessing problems or deficits
- providing information in unique ways
- identifying progress made
- giving feedback
- reinforcing learning
- evaluating learners' abilities

It's a JUNGLE out there...

- What type of beastly problems are we up against?
- Limited time
- Limited manpower
- Increasing self-care responsibilities
- Consumer expectations
- Lack of competence as educators

The Educator's Unique Position

- Successfully teaching people how to manage their own health is a true test and a most important function of professional nursing.
- As the largest group of health providers, nurses are in a unique position to "sell" good health habits to consumers.

Assessment of the learner includes attending to the three determinants of learning:

Learning Needs   (WHAT the learner needs to learn)

Readiness to Learn   (WHEN the learner is receptive to learning)

Learning Style   (HOW the learner best learns)

Haggard, 1989

Assessing Learning Needs

Assessment of Learning

- Identify the learner
- Choose the right setting
- Collect data on the learner
- Include the learner as a source of information
- Involve members of the health-care team
- Prioritize needs
- Determine the availability of educational resources
- Assess demands of the organization
- Take time-management issues into account

Needs are prioritized based on the following criteria:

- Mandatory—Needs which must be learned for survival when the learner's life or safety is threatened.
- Desirable—Needs which are not life-dependent but are related to well-being
- Possible—Needs for information which are "nice to know" but not essential or required because they are not directly related to daily activities or the particular situation of the learner.

Methods to Assess Learning Needs

- Informal conversations
- Structured interviews
- Focus groups
- Self-Administered questionnaires
- Tests
- Observations
- Patient charts

Assessing Learning Needs of Nursing Staff

- Written job descriptions
- Formal and informal requests
- Quality assurance reports
- Chart audits
- Rules and regulations
- Knox Four-Step approach

- Take **TIME** to take a **PEEK** at the four types of Readiness to Learn!

The Four Types of Readiness to Learn are:

- **P** = Physical readiness

- **E** = Emotional readiness

- **E** = Experiential readiness

- **K** = Knowledge readiness

Lichtenthal, 1990

1. **Physical** readiness
   - measures of ability
   - complexity of task
   - health status
   - gender
   - anxiety level
   - support system
2. **Emotional** readiness
   - Anxiety level
   - Support system
   - motivation
   - risk taking behavior
   - frame of mind
   - developmental stage
3. **Experiential** readiness
   - level of aspiration
   - past coping mechanisms
   - cultural background
   - locus of control
   - orientation
4. **Knowledge** readiness
   - present knowledge base
   - cognitive ability
   - learning disabilities

Learning Styles

Six Learning Style Principles

- Both the style by which the teacher prefers to teach and the style by which the student prefers to learn can be identified.
- Teachers need to guard against overteaching by their own preferred learning styles.
- Teachers are most helpful when they assist students in identifying and learning through the students' own style preferences.

Notes

Six Learning Style Principles

- Students should have the opportunity to learn through their preferred style.
- Students should be encouraged to diversify their style preferences.
- Teachers can develop specific learning activities that reinforce each style

---

Learning Style Instruments

- Brain Preference Indicator
  (Right-Brain, Left-Brain and Whole-Brain)
- Embedded Figures Test (EFT)
  (Field-Independent/Field-Dependent)
- Environmental Preference Survey (EPS)
  (Dunn and Dunn Learning Style Inventory)
- Myers-Briggs Type Indicator (MBTI)

Learning Style Instruments

- Gregorc Style Delineator
- Kolb Learning Style Inventory (LSI)
- 4MAT System
- Gardner's Seven Types of Intelligence

Right-Brain/Left-Brain and Whole-Brain Thinking

- Brain Preference Indicator
- Right hemisphere—emotional, visual-spatial, non-verbal hemisphere
  Thinking processes using the right-brain are intuitive, subjective, relational, holistic, and time free
- Left hemisphere—vocal and analytical side
  Thinking process using reality-based and logical thinking with verbalization

Right-Brain/Left-Brain and Whole-Brain Thinking

- No correct or wrong side of the brain
- Each hemisphere gathers in the same sensory information but handles the information in different ways
- Knowledge of one's own brain hemispherical performance can aid educators in identifying their strengths and weaknesses in teaching methods

Examples of Right-Brain/Left-Brain and Whole-Brain Thinking

- **Left Brain**
  - Prefers talking and writing
  - Recognizes/remembers names
  - Solves problems by breaking them into parts
  - Conscious of time and schedules

- **Right Brain**
  - Prefers drawing and manipulating objects
  - Recognizes/remembers faces
  - Solves problems by looking at the whole, looks for patterns, using hunches
  - Not conscious of time and schedules

  Whole brain - combining both sides of the brain

Field-Independent/Field-Dependent Embedded Figures Test

- Embedded Figures Test
- Learners have preference styles for certain environmental cues.
- Helpful in assisting the educator to structure the learning task and environment.
- Helpful in assessing the extent to which learners are able to ignore distractions from other persons.
- Assessing if learners see the whole first or the individual parts of a task when learning

Environment Preference Survey (LSI)

- Stimuli
  - Environmental
  - Emotional
  - Sociological
  - Physical
  - Psychological

Myers-Briggs Type Indicator

Extraversion (E) ⟺ Introversion (I)

Sensing (S) ⟺ Intuition (N)

Thinking (T) ⟺ Feeling (F)

Judgment (J) ⟺ Perception (P)

Kolb Learning Style Inventory
Perception Dimension

Concrete experience   Abstract conceptualization

Process Dimension

Active experimentation   Reflective observation

Diverger	Converger
Assimilator	Accommodator

Gregorc Style Delineator

PERCEPTION { Concrete / Abstract

CR

CS

AS

ORDERING { Sequential / Random

AR

4MAT System

- Combination of kolb's model combined with right/left brain research.
- Four types of learners.
- Educators can address all four learning styles by teaching sequentially from type one learner to type two learner, etc.
- Learning sequence is circular and cyclic.

Gardner's Seven Types of Intelligence

- Linguistic intelligence
- Spatial intelligence
- Body kinesthetic intelligence
- Interpersonal intelligence
- Musical intelligence
- Logical-mathematical intelligence
- Intrapersonal intelligence

Recent Discoveries About Learning Styles

- Understanding cognitive processes promotes optimal learning
- Learning style theories are applicable to novice-to-expert concept
- Expertise in a subject requires mastery of knowledge in a specific domain
- Learning is the process by which novices become experts

Interpretation of Use of Style Instruments

- Caution must be exercised in assessing styles so as not to ignore other equally important factors in learning
- Styles only describe how individuals process stimuli not how much or how well information is learned
- Style instruments should be selected based on reliability, validity, and the population for which they are to be used
- More than one learning style instrument should be used for appropriate assessment of learner

Notes

Chapter 5

Teaching Strategies Specific to
Developmental Stages of Life

Developmental Characteristics

- Chronological age versus stage of
  development
- Example: children with chronic illness
  often are delayed developmentally; an
  adolescent that suffers a traumatic event
  may regress developmentally.

Developmental Characteristics (cont'd)

- Rationale: Chronological age per se is not a
  good predictor of learning ability. At any
  given age, there can be a wide variation in
  physical, cognitive, and psychosocial
  variables. Developmental stage
  acknowledges that human growth and
  development are sequential, but not always
  specifically age-related.

Developmental Stages of Childhood

- Infancy and Toddlerhood
- Preschooler
- School-aged Child
- Adolescence
- Pedagogy is the art and science of helping children learn

Infancy and Toddlerhood

- Piaget: sensorimotor stage
  - Learning is through sensory experiences and through movement and manipulation of objects
- Erikson: trust vs. mistrust (birth to 12 months) autonomy vs. shame and doubt (1–3 years)
  - Building trust and learning to control willful desires

Infancy and Toddlerhood (cont'd)

- General Characteristics
  - Cognitive
    - Example: responds to step-by-step commands; language skills develop rapidly during this stage
  - Psychosocial
    - Example: routines provide sense of security

Infancy and Toddlerhood (cont'd)

- Teaching Strategies
  - Focus on normal development, safety, and wellness care
  - Use repetition and imitation
  - Stimulate the senses
  - Provide safety
  - Allow for play and manipulation of objects

Preschooler

- Piaget: preoperational stage
  - Egocentric; thinking is literal and concrete; precausal thinking
- Erikson: initiative vs. guilt
  - Taking on tasks for the sake of being involved and on the move; learning to express feelings through play

Preschooler (cont'd)

- General Characteristics
  - Cognitive
    - Example: animistic thinking; limited sense of time; egocentric; transductive reasoning
  - Psychosocial
    - Example: separation anxiety; play is his/her work; fears bodily injuries; active imagination

Preschooler (cont'd)

- Teaching Strategies
  - Build trust
  - Allow for manipulation of objects
  - Use positive reinforcement
  - Encourage questions
  - Provide simple drawings and stories
  - Focus on play therapy
  - Stimulate the senses

School-Aged Child

- Piaget: concrete operations stage
  - Developing logical thought processes and ability to reason syllogistically; understands cause and effect
- Erikson: industry vs. inferiority
  - Gaining a sense of responsibility and reliability; increased susceptibility to social forces outside the family unit; gaining awareness of uniqueness of special talents and qualities

School-Aged Child (cont'd)

- General Characteristics
  - Cognitive
    - Example: learns to draw conclusions and are able to understand cause and effect
  - Psychosocial
    - Example: fears failure and being left out of groups; fears illness and disability

School-Aged Child (cont'd)

- Teaching Strategies
  - Encourage independence
  - Use logical explanations and analogies
  - Relate to child's experience
  - Use subject-centered focus
  - Use play therapy
  - Provide group activities
  - Use drawings, models, dolls, painting, audio- and video-tapes

Adolescence

- Piaget: formal operations stage
  - Abstract thought; reasoning is both inductive and deductive
- Erikson: identity vs. role confusion
  - Struggling to establish own identity; seeking independence and autonomy

Adolescence (cont'd)

- General Characteristics
  - Cognitive
    - Example: abstract thinking; complex logical reasoning; can build on past experiences

Adolescence (cont'd)

- General Characteristics (cont'd)
  - Psychosocial
    - Example: *personal fable*—feels invulnerable, invincible/immune to natural laws
    - Example: *imaginary audience*—intense personal preoccupation

Adolescence (cont'd)

- Teaching Strategies
  - Establish trust
  - Identify control focus
  - Use peers for support and influence
  - Negotiate for change, contract
  - Focus on details
  - Make information meaningful to life

Adolescence (cont'd)

- Teaching Strategies (cont'd)
  - Ensure confidentiality and privacy
  - Use audiovisuals, role play, contracts, and reading materials
  - Allow for experimentation and flexibility within safe limits

Developmental Stages of Adulthood

- Young Adulthood
- Middle-Aged Adulthood
- Older Adulthood
- Andragogy: the art and science of helping adults learn
- Adult Learning Principles: relates learning to immediate needs; self-directed; teacher is facilitator; learner desires active role

Young Adulthood

- Piaget: formal operations stage (begins in adolescence and carries through adulthood)
  - Abstract thought; reasoning is both inductive and deductive
- Erikson: intimacy vs. isolation
  - Focusing on relationships and commitment to others in their personal, occupational, and social lives

Young Adulthood (cont'd)

- General Characteristics
  - Cognitive
    - Example: cognitive capacity is fully developed, but continuing to accumulate new knowledge and skills
  - Psychosocial
    - Example: autonomous; independent; stress related to the many decisions being made regarding career, marriage, parenthood and higher education

Notes

Notes

Young Adulthood (cont'd)

- Teaching Strategies
  - Use problem-centered focus
  - Draw on meaningful experiences
  - Focus on immediacy of application
  - Allow for self-direction and setting own pace
  - Organize material
  - Encourage role play

Middle-Aged Adulthood

- Piaget: formal operations stage
  - Abstract thought; reasoning is both inductive and deductive
- Erikson: generativity vs. self-absorption and stagnation
  - Reflecting on accomplishments and determining if life changes are needed

Middle-Aged Adulthood (cont'd)

- General Characteristics
  - Cognitive
    - Example: ability to learn remains steady throughout this stage
  - Psychosocial
    - Example: facing issues with grown children, changes in own health, and increased responsibility for own parents

Middle-Aged Adulthood (cont'd)

- Teaching Strategies
  - Maintain independence and reestablish normal life patterns
  - Assess positive and negative past learning experiences
  - Assess potential sources of stress
  - Provide information relative to life concerns and problems

Older Adulthood

- Piaget: formal operations stage
  - Abstract thought; reasoning is both inductive and deductive
- Erikson: ego integrity vs. despair
  - Coping with reality of aging, mortality, and reconciliation with past failures
- Geragogy—the teaching of older persons, accomodating the normal physical, cognitive and psychosocial changes

Older Adulthood (cont'd)

- General Characteristics
  - cognitive
    - Example: *fluid intelligence*—capacity to perceive relationships, to reason, and to perform abstract thinking, which declines with aging
    - Example: *crystallized intelligence*—the intelligence absorbed over a lifetime, which increases with experience

Notes

Older Adulthood (cont'd)

- Salient Characteristics (cont'd)
  - Psychosocial
    - Example: adjusting to changes in lifestyle, and physical limitations

Older Adulthood (cont'd)

- Teaching Strategies
  - Use concrete examples
  - Build on past experiences
  - Focus on one concept at a time
  - Use a slow pace
  - Use repetition and reinforcement
  - Provide brief explanations
  - Use analogies

Older Adulthood (cont'd)

- Teaching Strategies (cont'd)
  - Speak slowly and clearly
  - Use low-pitched tones
  - Minimize distractions
  - Rely on visual aids and supplement with verbal instructions
  - Use large letters and well-spaced print
  - Provide a safe environment
  - Give time to reminisce

Role of Family in Patient Education

- Family is a key variable influencing patient outcomes
- JCAHO accreditation standards require family participation
- The family can be the nurse's greatest ally
- It is important to choose the most appropriate caregiver to receive information

Summary

- Readiness to learn in children is subject-centered and motivation to learn in adults is problem-centered
- Rate of learning and capacity for learning, as well as situational and emotional barriers to learning, vary according to stages of development

Summary (cont'd)

- Knowledge of tasks associated with each developmental stage will help individualize the approach to education in meeting the needs and desires of learners and their families

Notes

_____
_____
_____
_____
_____
_____
_____
_____
_____
_____
_____
_____
_____
_____
_____
_____

Summary (cont'd)

- Nurses, as the main source of health education, must determine what needs to be taught, when to teach, how to teach, and who should be the focus of teaching in light of the developmental stage of the learner

_____
_____
_____
_____
_____
_____
_____
_____
_____
_____
_____
_____
_____
_____
_____
_____
_____
_____
_____
_____
_____
_____
_____
_____

Chapter 6: Motivation, Compliance and Health Behaviors of the Learner

Notes

Chapter 6

Motivation, Compliance, and Health
Behaviors of the Learner

Definition of Motivation

- Motivation: to set into motion, from the Latin word *Movere*; a psychological force that moves a person toward some kind of action, positive or negative.
- Motivation to learn is a willingness on the part of the learner to embrace learning, with readiness to learn as evidence of motivation.

Motivation

- Movement in the direction of meeting a need or reaching a goal
- All behavior is not motivated

Notes

Motivational Factors

- Personal attributes
- Environmental influences
- Relationship systems

Motivational Axioms

- Moderate anxiety is optimum for learning
- Learner readiness
- Setting realistic goals
- Learner satisfaction/success
- Uncertainty reduction or maintenance

Parameters of Assessment of Motivation

- Cognitive variables
- Affective variables
- Physiological variables
- Experiential variables
- Environmental variables
- Educator-learner relationship system

Cognitive Variables

- Capacity to learn
- Readiness to learn
  - Expressed self determination
  - Constructive attitude
  - Expressed desire and curiosity
  - Willingness to contract for behavioral outcomes

Affective Variables

- Expressions of constructive emotional state
- Moderate level of anxiety (optimum state)

Physiological Variables

- Capacity to perform required behavior

Experiential Variables

- Previous successful experiences

Environmental Variables

- Appropriateness of physical environment
- Social support systems
  - Family
  - Group
  - Work
  - Community resources

Educator-Learner Relationship System

- Prediction of positive relationship

Motivational Strategies

- Incentives, either intrinsically or extrinsically generated, are appeals or inducements to motivation.
- In the educational situation, reducing or eliminating barriers to achieve goals helps to instill or maintain motivation

Motivational Strategies (cont'dý)

- Clarify directions and expectations
- Make information meaningful to learner
- Manipulate environment to make it conducive to learning
- Provide positive verbal and nonverbal feedback
- Provide opportunities for success

Motivational/Models

- Maslow's Hierarchy of Needs
- ARCS Model
  - **A**ttention
  - **R**elevance
  - **C**onfidence
  - **S**atisfaction

Notes

Notes

Definition of Compliance Terminology

- **Compliance:** a submission or yielding to predetermined goals through regimens prescribed or established by others. As such, this term has a manipulative or authoritative undertone that infers an attempt to control the learner's right to decision-making.

Definition of Compliance Terminology (cont'd)

- **Adherence:** a commitment or attachment to a prescribed, predetermined regimen. This term is used interchangeably with compliance in the measurement of health outcomes.

Definition of Compliance Terminology (cont'd)

- **Noncompliance:** nonsubmission or resistance of an individual to follow a prescribed, predetermined regimen. As such, this term carries a negative connotation of the learner, but may in fact be a resilient response or defensive coping mechanism to a stressful situation.

Compliance/Adherence

- Is observable
- Can be measured
- Health care provider viewed as authority
- Learner viewed as submissive
- Refers to the ability to maintain health - promoting regimens
- Outcomes determined largely by health-care provider

Theoretical Perspective on Compliance

- Theories related to patient compliance with health care regimens:
- Biomedical
- Behavioral/social learning
- Communication feedback loop
- Rational belief
- Self-regulatory systems

Concepts Impacting on Compliance

- Locus of Control
- Functional illiteracy
- Noncompliance

Notes

Models/Theories for Health Behaviors of the Learner

- Health Belief Model
- Health Promotion Model
- Self-Efficacy Theory
- Theory of Reasoned Action
- The PRECEDE-PROCEED Model
- Therapeutic Alliance Model

Health Belief Model

- Predictor of preventive health behavior
  - Individual perceptions
  - Modifying factors
  - Likelihood of action

Health Promotion Model

- Uses approach behaviors rather than avoidance of disease behaviors
  - Individual characteristics and experiences
  - Behavior-specific cognitions and affect
  - Behavioral outcome

Self-Efficacy Theory

- Focuses on a person's expectations relative to a specific course of action
  - Mode of induction
  - Source of efficacy
  - Cognitive processes
  - Competency perceptions
  - Expected outcomes

Theory of Reasoned Action

- Focuses on prediction and understanding of human behavior within a social context
  - Beliefs
  - Attitudes and norms
  - Intention
  - Behavior

PRECEDE-PROCEED Model

- Uses an epidemiological perspective on health promotion
  - PRECEDE component identifies priorities and objectives
  - PROCEED component addresses criteria for policy, implementation, and evaluation

Therapeutic Alliance Model

- Compliance—Dependency
- Adherence—Conforming
- Therapeutic Alliance—Self Care

Selection of Model for Health Education

- Understand and compare models
- Educator beliefs and choice of model
- Functional utility of model

Nurse as Educator in Health Promotion

- Roles
  - Facilitator
  - Contractor
  - Organizer
  - Evaluator

Notes

Chapter 7

Literacy in the Adult Patient
Population

Definition of Terms

- **Literacy:** the ability of adults to read, write, and comprehend information at the 8th grade level or above.
- **Illiteracy:** the total inability of adults to read, write, and comprehend information.
- **Low Literacy:** the ability of adults to read, write, and comprehend information between the 5th to 8th grade level of difficulty. Also synonymous with the terms marginally literate or marginally illiterate.

Definition of Terms (cont'd)

- **Functionally Illiterate:** the inability of adults to read, write, and comprehend information below the 5th grade level of difficulty in order to use information as it is intended for effective functioning in today's society.
- **Readability:** the ease with which written or printed information can be read.

Definition of Terms (cont'd)

- **Comprehension:** the degree to which individuals understand and accurately interpret what they have read.
- **Numeracy:** the ability to read and interpret numbers.

Literacy Relative to Oral Instruction

- Little attention has been paid to the role of oral communication in the assessment of illiteracy.
- **Iloralacy:** the inability to comprehend simple oral language communicated through speaking of common vocabulary, phrases, or slang words.

Literacy Relative to Computer Instruction

- The ability to use computers for communication is an increasingly popular issue with respect to literacy of learner
- As an educational tool, the potential for computers is increasingly being realized and appreciated by health-care providers
- Computers are used to convey as well as to access information

Literacy Relative to Computer Instruction (cont'd)

- The opportunity to expand the knowledge base of learners through telecommunications requires nurse educators to attend to computer literacy levels
- The negative effects of illiteracy and low literacy in the use of computers is similar to the literacy issues with the use of printed materials and oral instruction.

Scope and Incidence of Literacy Problem

- The U.S. ranks only 49th from the top among 159 members in the United Nations in average national literacy level.
- Approximately 20–30 million Americans are considered illiterate and an additional 30–45 million Americans are low literate.
- That is, about 1/5 or 20% of the adult U.S. population lacks literacy skills needed to acquire knowledge to cope with the requirements of day-to-day living

Scope and Incidence of Literacy Problem (cont'd)

- Estimates of problem are conservative due to the difficulty in defining and testing literacy levels and because few people admit to being illiterate or low literate
- The mean literacy level of Americans is at or below the 8th grade
- The rates of illiteracy and low literacy are expected to continue to rise due to the increasing complexity of technological and informational demands

Notes

Factors Lending to Reduced Literacy Levels

- A rise in the number of immigrants
- The aging of our population
- The increasing complexity of information
- The added number of people living in poverty
- Changes in policies and funding for public education
- Disparity of opportunity between minority versus non-minority populations

Those at Risk

- The economically disadvantaged
- The elderly
- Immigrants (particularly illegal ones)
- High school dropouts
- Racial minorities
- The unemployed

Stereotypes and Myths

- Myth #1: people who are illiterate have below normal IQ's
- Myth #2: people who are illiterate can be recognized by their appearance
- Myth #3: the number of years of schooling completed correlates with literacy skills

Stereotypes and Myths (cont'd)

- Myth #4: people who are illiterate come from similar socioeconomic, racial, and ethnic minority backgrounds
- Myth #5: people who are illiterate freely admit to having problems with reading, writing and comprehension

Clues to Illiteracy

- Most people with limited literacy abilities are masters of concealment.
- Possible signs of poor or nonexistent reading ability include:
  - Reacting to complex learning situations by withdrawal or avoidance
  - Using the excuse of being too busy, not interested, too tired, or not feeling well enough to read instructional materials
  - Claiming they lost, forgot, or broke their glasses

Clues to Illiteracy (cont'd)

- Surrounding themselves with books, magazines, and newspapers to give the impression that they are able to read
- Insisting on reading the information at home or with a spouse or friend present
- Asking someone to read information for them
- Becoming nervous when asked to read
- Acting confused or talking out of context about the topic of conversation

Notes

Clues to Illiteracy (con't)

- Showing signs of frustration when attempting to read
- Having difficulty following directions
- Listening and watching attentively to try to memorize information
- Failing to ask questions
- Revealing a discrepancy between what they hear and what is written

Impact of Illiteracy on Motivation and Compliance

- People with poor literacy skills think in very concrete, specific, and literal terms
- Characteristics of thinking:
  - Disorganization of thought
  - Limited perception of ideas
  - Slow rate of vocabulary and language development
  - Poor problem-solving skills

Impact of Illiteracy on Motivation and Compliance (cont'd)

- Difficulty analyzing and synthesizing information
- Difficulty formulating questions
- Struggles handling more than one piece of information at a time

Impact of Illiteracy on Motivation and Compliance (cont'd)

- Cultural literacy involves the ability to understand nuances, information, slang and sarcasm
- Non-compliant behavior may be the result of not understanding what is expected rather than an unwillingness to follow instructions

Ethical and Legal Concerns

- Printed education materials (PEMs) that are too difficult to read or comprehend result in miscommunication between consumers and health care providers
- The JACHO requires that patients and their significant others are provided with information that is understandable
- The Patient's Bill of Rights mandates that patients receive complete and current information in terms they can understand

Ethical and Legal Concerns (cont'd)

- Informed consent, as a result of verbal and/or written instructions, must be voluntary and based on an understanding of benefits and risks to treatment or procedures
- Health care professionals are liable, legally and/or ethically, when information shared is above the level of the patient's ability to comprehend

Trends Increasing Need for Patient Education

- Early discharges
- Decreased reimbursement for direct care
- Increased delivery of care in home and community settings
- Greater demands on nursing personnel time
- Increased technological complexity of treatment
- Reliance on printed education materials to substitute for or supplement direct patient instruction

Readability of Printed Education Materials (PEMs)

- Research findings indicate that most PEMs are written at grade levels that far exceed the reading ability of the majority of patients
- The readability level of PEMs is between the 10th and 12th grade yet the average reading level of adults falls between the 5th and 8th grade.

Readability of Printed Education Materials (PEMs) (cont'd)

- People typically read at least two grades below their highest level of schooling
- PEMs serve no useful teaching purpose if patients are unable to understand them

Measurement Tools to Test Readability

- The most widely used standardized readability formulas rate high on reliability and predictive validity
- Formulas evaluate readability levels using the average length of sentences and the number of multi-syllabic words in a passage
- Computerized readability analysis has made evaluation of written materials quick and easy

Measurement Tools to Test Readability (cont'd)

- Readability formulas:
  1. **Spache Grade-Level Score**: this formula is unique because it evaluates materials written for children at elementary grades 1-3
  2. **Flesch formula**: measures materials written between the 5th grade and the college level

Measurement Tools to Test Readability (cont'd)

3. **Fog Index**: measures materials written between the 4th grade and the college level
4. **Fry Readability Graph**: measures materials written between the Ist grade and the college level
5. **SMOG formula**: measures materials written between 4th grade and the college level. Most popular because of its accuracy, speed, use, and simplicity.

Comprehension Tests

- **Cloze Procedureý**: specifically recommended for assessing health literature. Every 5th word is systematically deleted from a portion of a text and the reader has to fill in the blanks with the appropriate words.
- **Listening Test**: a passage, selected from instructional materials written at approximately the 5th grade level, is read aloud and then the listener is asked questions on key points relevant to the content.

Reading Skills Tests

1. **WRAT** (Wide Range Achievement Test): measures the ability of a person to correctly pronounce words from a graduated list of 100 words. It tests word recognition , not vocabulary or comprehension of text material.
2. **REALM** (Rapid Estimate of Adult Literacy in Medicine): measures a person's ability to read and pronounce medical and health-related vocabulary from three lists graduated in order from the most simple words to the most complex words.

Assessing Suitability of Instructional Materials

- **Suitability Assessment of Materials (SAM) instrument**: includes evaluation criteria to identify deficiencies in such factors as content, literacy demand, graphics, layout, typography and cultural appropriateness of print, illustration, video, and audio instructional materials.

Steps to Take Prior to Writing or Rewriting a Text

- Decide on what the learner should *do* or *know* (the outcome to be accomplished)
- Choose information that is relevant and needed to achieve behavioral objectives
- Select other forms of media to supplement written information
- Organize topics into logically sequenced chunks of information
- Determine the reading level of material and write the text 2–4 grades below the average reading grade-level score of the intended audience

Simplifying Readability of Printed Education Materials

- Elements such as technical format, concept demand, legibility, literacy level, and accuracy and clarity of a message also affects the readability of printed materials
- To reduce the discrepancy between the literacy demand of written materials and the reader's actual reading and comprehension skills, the nurse educator must attend to basic linguistic, motivational, organizational, and content principles

Techniques for Writing Effective Educational Materials

- Write in a conversational style with an active voice using the personal pronouns "you" and "your"
- Use short, familiar words with only one or two syllables
- Spell words out rather than using abbreviations or acronyms
- Use numbers and statistics only when necessary

Notes

Techniques for Writing Effective Educational Materials (cont'd)

- Keep sentences short, preferably 20 words or less
- Define any technical or unfamiliar words
- Use words consistently throughout text
- Use advance organizers
- Limit use of connective words
- Make the first sentence of a paragraph the topic sentence

Techniques for Writing Effective Educational Materials (cont'd)

- Reduce concept density by limiting each paragraph to a single message or action
- Include a summary paragraph to review key points of information
- use a question and answer format to present information simply and in conversational style
- Allow for plenty of white space for ease of reading and to reduce density of information

Techniques for Writing Effective Educational Materials (cont'd)

- Design layouts that gives direction to the reader
- Select simple type style (serif) and large font (14–18 print size). Avoid using *italics* and all CAPITAL letters
- Highlight important ideas or words with bold type or underlining
- Use color to emphasize key points and to organize topics

Techniques for Writing Effective Educational Materials (cont'd)

- Limit length of document to cover only essential information
- Select paper with non-glossy finish and color that contrasts with typeface (black print or white is most easily read)
- Use bold line drawings and simple diagrams for clarity of message

Teaching Strategies for Low-Literate Learners

- Establish a trusting relationship
- Use the smallest amount of information to achieve behavioral objectives
- Make points of information vivid and explicit
- Teach one step at a time
- Use multiple teaching methods and tools

Teaching Strategies for Low-Literate Learners (cont'd)

- Give learners the chance to restate information in their own words and to demonstrate procedures
- Keep motivation high by using praise and rewards
- Build in coordination of information and procedures by using techniques of tailoring and cuing
- Use repetition to reinforce information

Notes

Notes

Summary

- The ability to learn from instructional materials depends on the client's educational background, motivation, and reading and comprehension skills
- The prevalence of functional illiteracy and low literacy is a major problem in the U.S. adult population
- Nurse educators need to know how to identify clients with literacy problems, assess their needs, and choose appropriate interventions

Chapter 8: Gender, Socioeconomic and Cultural Attributes of the Learner

Notes

Chapter 8

Gender, Socioeconomic, and
Cultural Attributes of the Learner

Gender Differences

- Impact of genetics and environment
- Brain structure in males and females
- Brain functioning in males and females
  - Affective responses
  - Cognitive processing

Gender Differences (cont'd)

- Gender-related cognitive abilities
  - General intelligence
  - Verbal ability
  - Mathematical ability
  - Spatial ability
  - Problem solving
  - School achievement

Notes

Gender Differences (cont'd)

- Gender-related personality characteristics
  - Aggression
  - Conformity and dependence
  - Values and life goals
  - Achievement orientation

Gender Differences (cont'd)

- Teaching strategies
  - Males and females use different symbols, belief systems, and ways to express themselves, much in the same manner that different ethnic groups have distinct cultures
  - Although stereotypical, males and females have some general qualities that need to be taken into consideration when teaching

Socioeconomic Differences

- Variables affecting health status and health behaviors
  - Educational level
  - Family income
  - Family structure
- All three variables affect health beliefs, health practices, and readiness to learn

Socioeconomic Differences (cont'd)

- Social class
  - Types of indices for measurement
    - Occupation of parents
    - Income of family
    - Location of residence
    - Educational level of parents

Socioeconomic Differences (cont'd)

- Social class (cont'd)
  - Poverty circle—low education level results in occupations with lower levels of pay, prestige, and intellectual demand; families living at this level become part of the cycle that does not allow one to easily change a pattern of life.

Socioeconomic Differences (cont'd)

- Impact of socioeconomics on health
  - lack of financial resources have a negative impact on prevention of illness, compliance with treatment, and motivation to learn; focus is on day to day survival
- Impact of illness on socioeconomics
  - the cost of medical care and supplies can negatively impact a person's/family's financial well-being, especially if socioeconomic level is already low

Notes

Socioeconomic Differences (cont'd)

- Teaching strategies
  - Directed toward attaining and maintaining health
  - Focus on:
    - Avoiding health risks
    - Reducing illness episodes
    - Establishing healthful environmental conditions
    - How to access health-care services

Cultural Differences

- Definition of cultural terms
  - Minority groups
  - Historically underrepresented groups
  - Culturological assessment
  - Culture
  - Ethnicity
  - Ethnocentrism

Cultural Differences (cont'd)

- Definition of cultural terms (cont'd)
  - Cultural relativism
  - Cultural assessment
  - Acculturation
  - Transcultural nursing
  - Ethnomedical

Cultural Differences Continued

- Culturally sensitive care
  - Six cultural phenomena
    - Communication
    - Personal space
    - Social organization
    - Time
    - Environmental control
    - Biological variations

Cultural Differences (cont'd)

- Culturally sensitive care continued
  - Four steps to providing culturally sensitive care
    - Examine personal culture
    - Familiarity with client culture
    - Identify adaptations made by client
    - Modify client teaching based on data from earlier steps

Cultural Differences (cont'd)

- Cultural assessment
  - Nurse-client negotiations model
    - Popular arena
    - Professional arena
    - Folk arena

Cultural Differences (cont'd)

- Cultural assessment (cont'd)
  - Culturally competent model of care
    - Cultural competence
    - Cultural awareness
    - Cultural knowledge
    - Cultural skill
    - Cultural encounters

Cultural Differences (cont'd)

- General assessment and teaching strategies
  - Establish rapport
  - Assessment
    - Readiness to learn, considering cultural background
    - Determine health beliefs, values, and practices
  - Use client's primary language

Cultural Differences (cont'd)

- Four major culture groups
  - Latin American Culture
  - Black American Culture
  - Asian/Pacific Culture
  - Native American Culture

Latin American Culture

- Characteristics
  - Economically disadvantaged
  - Strong family ties
  - Get a lot of information from mass media
  - Spanish or english may be primary language
  - Categorize disease into "hot" and "cold", magical origin, emotional origin, folk-defined, or "standard scientific"

Latin American Culture (cont'd)

- Teaching Strategies
  - Encourage involvement in teaching/learning
  - Provide adequate space for extended family
  - Incorporate religious beliefs into plan
  - Respect cultural values and take time to learn beliefs
  - Be considerate of feelings of modesty

Latin American Culture (cont'd)

- Teaching Strategies (cont'd)
  - Determine primary language
  - Avoid slang
  - Do not assume understanding
  - Use of interpreter
  - Provide written materials in Spanish

Notes

Black American Culture

- Characteristics
  - Many acculturated into american "way of life"
  - Disadvantaged due to poverty and lack of education
  - Extended family important and elders hold highest respect
  - Strong religious values

Black American Culture (cont'd)

- Characteristics (cont'd)
  - Voodoo
  - Believe all animate and inanimate objects have good or evil spirits
  - Folk remedies
  - Witchcraft

Black American Culture (cont'd)

- Teaching strategies
  - Any folk practices or religious beliefs should be respected and allowed (if not harmful) and incorporated into the recommended treatment

Asian/Pacific Culture

- Characteristics
  - Blend of four philosophies
    - Buddhism
    - Confucianism
    - Taoism
    - Phi
  - Male authority

Asian/Pacific Culture (cont'd)

- Characteristics (cont'd)
  - "Saving face" (conduct as a result of a sense of pride)
  - Strong family ties
  - Respect for parents, elders, teachers, and authority figures

Asian/Pacific Culture (cont'd)

- Teaching Strategies
  - Friendly, non-threatening approach
  - Give permission to ask questions
  - Consider language barriers
  - Learning style is passive
  - Learning by repetition and rote memorization

Asian/Pacific Culture (cont'd)

- Teaching strategies (cont'd)
  - Need reassurance
  - Ask questions in different ways to assure understanding

Native American Culture

- Characteristics
  - Spiritual attachment to the land
  - Intimacy of religion and medicine
  - Strong ties to family/tribe
  - View children as an asset, not a liability
  - Believe supernatural powers exist in animate and inanimate objects
  - Avoid acculturation

Native American Culture (cont'd)

- Characteristics (cont'd)
  - Lack materialism, time consciousness, and desire to share with others
  - Believe witchcraft is cause of illness
  - Not very future oriented
  - Do not feel they have control over their destiny
  - Looking into another's eyes reveals and may steal someone's soul

Native American Culture (cont'd)

- Teaching strategies
  - Focus on giving information about diseases and risk factors
  - Emphasize teaching of skills related to changes in diet and exercise
  - Consider each tribe's unique customs and language

Summary

- Gender, socioeconomic status and cultural background impact teaching and learning
- It is important to recognize that there are differences among groups and individuals

Summary (cont'd)

- The nurse should not stereotype or generalize common characteristics of a group to all members associated with that group

Notes

Chapter 9

Special Populations

Developmental or Acquired Disabilities

- Sensory
- Cognitive
- Physical

Definition of Terms

- **Habilitation:** includes all activities/ interactions that enable an individual with a disability to develop new abilities to achieve his or her maximum potential.
- **Rehabilitation:** the relearning of previous skills, which often requires an adjustment to altered functional abilities and altered lifestyle.

Americans with Disabilities Act (ADA)

- Enacted in 1990, this legislation has extended civil rights protection to millions of Americans who are disabled. The ADA defines a disability as a physical or mental impairment which substantially limits one or more of the major life activities of the individual.

The Nurse's Role in Assessment of Client Needs

- Nature of problem
- Short and long-term consequences of a disability
- Coping mechanisms
- Type and extent of deficits
- Extent of client's knowledge deficits
- Client's readiness to learn
- Client's support system

Types of Disabilities

- Sensory deficits
- Learning disabilities
- Physical disabilities
- Communication disorders
- Chronic illness

Sensory Deficits: Hearing Impairments

- Any type of hearing loss (complete loss or reduction in sensitivity to sounds), the etiology of which may be related to either a conduction or sensory-neural problem
- 1.8 million Americans are deaf and an additional 10% of people (26 million) have some degree of hearing loss

Hearing Impairments (cont'd)

- Etiology: congenital defect, trauma, or disease
- Factors Affecting Communication
  a. degree of hearing loss
  b. how long impaired

Hearing Impairments (con't)

- Modes of Communication to Facilitate
- Teaching/Learning:
  a. American Sign Language (ASL)
  b. Lip reading
  c. Written materials
  d. Verbalization by client
  e. Sound augmentation
  f. Telecommunication devices for the deaf (TDD)

General Guidelines for Teaching

- Use natural speech patterns; do not over articulate
- Use simple sentences
- Get attention of client by light touch on arm
- Face client, standing no more than 6 feet away

General Guidelines for Teaching (cont'd)

- Avoid standing in front of bright light, which obscures your face
- Minimize motions of head while speaking
- Refrain from placing IV in hand client needs for sign language

Sensory Deficits: Visual Impairments

- **Legal Blindness:** defined as vision of 20/200 or less in the better eye with correction or if visual field limits in both eyes are within 20 degrees diameter
- More than 2.5 million Americans over age 65 are severely impaired
- Etiology: infection, trauma, poisoning, congenital, degeneration

Visual Impairments (cont'd)

- Factors influencing functionality
  a. Degree of impairment
  b. How long impaired
- Common eye diseases of aging
  a. Macular degeneration
  b. Cataracts
  c. Glaucoma
  d. Diabetic retinopathy

General Guidelines for Teaching

- Secure services of low-vision specialist to obtain adaptive optical devices
- Avoid tendency to shout and to use nonverbal cues
- Always announce your presence and identify yourself
- Allow client to touch, handle, and manipulate equipment

General Guidelines for Teaching (cont'd)

- Be descriptive in explaining procedures
- Use large font size for printed or handwritten materials
- Avoid color; rely on black and white for printed materials
- Use alternative instructional tools that stimulate auditory and tactile senses

Learning Disabilities

- Heterogeneous group of disorders of listening, speaking, reading, writing, reasoning or mathematical abilities
- Other Terms for Learning Disability
  - Minimal brain dysfunction
  - Attention Deficit Disorder (ADD)
  - Dyslexia
  - Hyperactivity

Learning Disabilities (cont'd)

- Approximately 10–15% of American population are learning disabled
- Majority have language, integrative processing, or memory deficits
- Most have normal or superior intelligence

Categories of Learning Disabilities

- **Input disabilities**
  - Difficulty receiving and recording information in brain
  - Types of input disabilities
    - Visual perceptual disorders
    - Auditory perceptual disorders
    - Integrative processing disorders
    - Short-term or long-term memory disorders

Categories of Learning Disabilities (cont'd)

- **Output disabilities**
  - Difficulty responding orally and/or performing physical tasks
  - Types of output disabilities
    - Language disorders
    - Motor disorders

Categories of Learning Disabilities (cont'd)

- **Attention deficit disorder**
  - Three main subtypes
  - Characteristics
    - Inattention
    - Impulsiveness
    - Difficulty with time management

General Teaching Strategies for Clients with Learning Disabilities

- Eliminate distractions; provide quiet environment
- Conduct individualized assessment to determine how client learns best
- Adapt teaching methods and tools to client's preferred learning style
- Ask questions of parents about accommodations needed when client is child

General Teaching Strategies (cont'd)

- Use repetition to reinforce messages
- Ask client to repeat or demonstrate what was learned to clear up any possible misconceptions
- Use brief but frequent teaching sessions to increase retention and recall of information
- Encourage client's active participation

Physical Disabilities

- Brain injury
  - Trauma causes changes in behavior, personality, and/or cognitive ability
  - It occurs most frequently in adolescent and young adults
  - Cognitive defecits may include poor attention span, slower processing, confusion, loss of memory, distractability, impulsiveness, difficulty problem solving

Brain Injury

- General teaching strategies
  - Conduct family group sessions
  - Focus on client safety and family coping
  - Give step-by-step instructions
  - Allow time for responses
  - Provide small amounts of information
  - Keep sessions short

Communication Disorders

- Deficits affect perceptual and/or language abilities
- Most common residual communication deficits
  - Expressive aphasia
  - Receptive aphasia
  - Dysarthria

General Teaching Strategies for Clients with Aphasia

- Encourage and praise participation
- Acknowledge client's frustrations
- Keep distractions to a minimum
- Speak slowly using normal tone and short sentences

General Teaching Strategies for Clients with Aphasia

- Have only one person speak at a time
- Stand where client can see your face
- Check to be sure each message is understood
- Allow person time to respond

Notes

General Teaching Strategies for Clients with Dysarthria

- Ensure quiet environment
- Encourage concentration and intention to improve speech clarity
- Ask questions that need only short replies
- Use alternative methods of communication
- Encourage client to speak slower and louder
- Do not simplify message since the client's comprehension not affected

Chronic Illness

- Is permanent
- Affects every aspect of life—physical, social, psychological, economic and spiritual
- Successful management is life-long process

Chronic Illness

- Development of good learning skills is a matter of survival
- Learning process must begin with onset of illness
- Often conflict between feelings of dependence and need for independence

General Teaching Strategies

- Acknowledge loss or change in roles
- Recognize effects of illness on self-esteem
- Emphasize regimens that match physical strength
- Individualize instruction relevant to problems encountered
- Encourage integration of new knowledge for problem-solving

Impact of Chronic Illness or Disability on Family

A. Family Role Adjustments
B. Family Participation in Teaching and Learning

Adaptive Computing

- Refers to the professional services and the hardware and software that make computer technology accessible to persons with disabilities
- Impact on lives of disabled persons
  - Has liberated people with disabilities from social isolation and feelings of helplessness
  - Enables independence leading to increase in feelings of self-worth

Adaptive Computing (con't)

– Benefits persons with almost any type of disability
- Advocacy role of nurses
  – Recommend clients use computer technology
  – Assist in obtaining appropriate equipment and training
- Types of adaptations available

Summary

- Disability has tremendous impact on lives of clients and their families
- Successful habilitation or rehabilitation means acquiring and applying new knowledge and skills
- The nurse as teacher needs to be well prepared to help clients learn to live independently

Notes

Chapter 10

Behavioral Objectives

Characteristics of Goals and Objectives

- Definition of Terms
- **Goals:** the final outcome of what is achieved at the end of the teaching-learning process
- **Objective:** a behavior describing the performance learners should be able to exhibit to be considered competent

---

Characteristics of Goals and Objectives (cont'd)

- **Educational/Instructional Objectives:** content-oriented, teacher-centered outcomes of the education process in reference to an aspect of a program or a total program of study
- **Behavioral/learning Objectives:** action-oriented, learner-centered outcomes of the teaching/learning process

Differences Between Goals and Objectives

Goals	Objectives
global	specific
broad	singular
long-term	short-term

Responsibility for Establishing Goals and Objectives

- Setting of goals and objectives must be a mutual decision-making process between the teacher and the learner
- Both parties must "buy into" and participate in establishing predetermined objectives and goals prior to initiating the teaching/learning process
- Blending what the learner wants to learn and what the teacher has assessed the learner needs to know provides for a mutually accountable, respectful, and fulfilling educational experience

The Debate About Using Behavioral Objectives

- **Arguments for**
  - Keeps teaching learner-centered
  - Communicates plan to others
  - Helps learners stay on track
  - Organizes educational approach
  - Ensures process is deliberate
  - Tailors teaching to learner's needs
  - Focuses attention on learner
  - Orients teacher and learner to outcomes

Three Major Advantages to Writing Objectives

- Provides basis for selection and design of instructional content, methods, and materials
- Provides learner with means to organize efforts toward accomplishing objectives
- Allows for determination as to the extent objectives have been accomplished

Writing Behavioral Objectives

- Three important characteristics
    1. **Performance**—describes what the learner is expected to be able to do
    2. **Condition**—describes the situation under which behavior will be observed
    3. **Criterion**—describes how well or with what accuracy the learner must be able to perform

The STP Approach

- A simple mnemonic to remember the components of a well-written behavioral objective is:
    1. **S**tudent behavior (performance)
    2. **T**esting situation (condition)
    3. **P**erformance level (criterion)

Notes

Common Mistakes When Writing Objectives

- Describing what the instructor rather than the learner will do
- Including more than one behavior in a single objective
- Forgetting to include all three characteristics
- Using performance terms that are not action-oriented and are difficult to measure

Common Mistakes (cont'd)

- Writing an unattainable, unrealistic objective
- Writing objectives unrelated to stated goal
- Cluttering an objective with unnecessary information
- Making an objective too general so that the outcome is not clear

Taxonomy of Objectives

- Behavior is defined according to type (domain category) and level of complexity (simple to complex).
- **Three Types of Learning Domains**
  1. Cognitive—the "thinking" domain
  2. Affective—the "feeling" domain
  3. Psychomotor—the "skills" domain

Complexity of Domain Levels

- Objectives in each domain are classified in a taxonomic form of hierarchy into low (most simple), medium (moderately difficult), and high (most complex) levels of behavior.
- **Cognitive Levels**
  - Knowledge ⟶ evaluation
- **Affective Levels**
  - Receiving ⟶ characterization
- **Psychomotor**
  - Perception ⟶ origination

Teaching in the Cognitive Domain

- Learning in this domain involves acquisition of information based on the learner's intellectual abilities and thinking processes.
- Methods most often used to stimulate learning in the cognitive domain include:
  - Lecture
  - One-to-one instruction
  - Computer-assisted instruction

Teaching in the Cognitive Domain (cont'd)

- Cognitive domain learning is the traditional focus of most teaching
- Cognitive knowledge is an essential prerequisite for learning affective and psychomotor skills

Notes

Teaching in the Affective Domain

- Learning in this domain involves commitment to feelings; the degree to which feelings or attitudes are incorporated into one's personality or value system
- Methods most often used to stimulate learning in the affective domain include:
  - Group discussion
  - Role-playing

Teaching in the Affective Domain (cont'd)

  - Role-modeling
  - Simulation gaming
  - Questioning
- Nurses are encouraged to attend to the needs of the whole person by recognizing that learning is subjective and values driven
- More time in teaching needs to focus on exploring and clarifying learner feelings, emotions, and attitudes

Teaching in the Psychomotor Domain

- Learning in this domain involves acquiring fine and gross motor abilities with increasing complexity of neuromuscular coordination.
- Methods most often used to stimulate learning in the psychomotor domain include:
  - Demonstration
  - Return demonstration
  - Simulation
  - Gaming
  - Self-instruction

Teaching in the Psychomotor Domain (cont'd)

- Psychomotor skill development is very egocentric and requires learner concentration
- Asking questions that demand a cognitive or affective response during psychomotor learning interferes with psychomotor performance
- The ability to perform a skill is not equivalent to learning a skill
- "Practice makes perfect"—repetition leads to perfection and reinforcement of behavior

Factors Influencing Psychomotor Skill Acquisition

- The amount of practice required to learn a new skill varies with the individual depending upon such things as:
  - Readiness to learn
  - Motivation to learn
  - Past experience
  - Health status

Factors Influencing Psychomotor Skill Acquisition (cont'd)

- Environmental stimuli
- Anxiety level
- Developmental stage
- Practice session length

Development of Teaching Plans

- Predetermined goals and objectives serve as a basis for developing a teaching plan
- Mutually agreed upon goals and objectives clarify what the learner is to learn and what the teacher is to teach

Reasons to Construct Teaching Plans

1. Ensures a logical approach to teaching and keeps instruction on target.
2. Communicates in writing an action plan for the learner, teacher, and other providers to follow.
3. Serves as a legal document that indicates a plan is in place and the extent of progress toward implementation.

Basic Elements of a Teaching Plan

- Purpose
- Goal statement
- Objectives (subobjectives)
- Content outline
- Methods of teaching
- Time allotment
- Resources for instruction
- Evaluation

The Major Criterion for Judging a Teaching Plan

- **Internal consistency** exists when you can answer "yes" to the following questions:
  - Does the plan facilitate a relationship between its parts?
  - Do all 8 elements of the plan "hang together"?

The Major Criterion for Judging a Teaching Plan (cont'd)

  - Is the identified domain of learning in each objective reflected in the purpose and goal as well as across the plan all the way through to the end process of evaluation?

The Concept of Learning Curve

- Learning Curve: A graphic depiction of changes in psychomotor performance at different stages of practice during a specified time period
  - Six stages of the theoretical learning curve
  - The irregularity of individual learning curves

Notes

Summary

- Assessment of the learner is a prerequisite to formulating objectives.
- Writing clear and concise behavioral objectives is fundamental to the education process.
- Goals and objectives serve as a guide to planning, implementation, and evaluation of teaching and learning.

Notes

Chapter 11

Teaching Methods and Instructional Settings

Teaching Methods

- Definition
  - Techniques or approaches that the teacher uses to bring the learner in contact with the content to be learned

Teaching Methods

- Lecture
- Group Discussion
- One-to-One Teaching
- Demonstration
- Return Demonstration
- Gaming
- Simulation

Lecture

- Definition
  - A teaching method in which the nurse verbally transmits information directly to groups of learners for the purpose of education. It is highly structured.

Lecture

- Advantages
  - Cost effective
  - Targets large groups
  - Useful for cognitive domain learning
- Limitations
  - Not individualized
  - Passive learners

Group Discussion

- Definition
  - A teaching method in which patients are together to exchange information and feelings with each other and the nurse to achieve educational objectives.

Group Discussion

- Advantages
  - Stimulates sharing of ideas and emotions
  - Active learners
  - Useful for cognitive and affective domains of learning
- Limitations
  - Shy member does not participate
  - Dominant member overwhelms the group
  - Highly diverse groups may have difficulty interacting

One-to-One Teaching

- Definition
  - A teaching method in which the nurse delivers individual instruction to a patient

One-to-One Teaching

- Advantages
  - Active learner
  - Tailored to individual's needs and goals
  - Useful for all three learning domains
- Limitations
  - Can be expensive because it is labor intensive
  - Isolates learner

Notes

Notes

Demonstration

- Definition
  - A teaching method in which the learner is shown by the teacher how to perform a particular skill.

Demonstration

- Advantages
  - Previews exact skill for the learner
  - Useful for psychomotor domain learning
- Limitations
  - May be expensive because all learners need to easily visualize skill. This requires small groups or individual teaching.

Return Demonstration

- Definition
  - A teaching method in which the learner attempts to perform a skill with cues from the teacher as needed.

Return Demonstration

- Advantages
  - Active learner
  - Individual guidance
  - Useful for psychomotor domain learning
- Limitations
  - Labor intensive to view individual performance

Gaming

- Definition
  - A teaching method requiring the learner to participate in a competitive activity with preset rules to achieve an educational objective.

Gaming

- Advantages
  - Active learner
  - Perceived as "fun" by many learners
  - Useful for all three domains of learning
- Limitations
  - Too competitive for some learners

Simulation

- Definition
  - A teaching method requiring creation of a hypothetical or artificial experience to engage the patient in an activity that reflects real-life conditions without the risk-taking consequences of an actual experience

Simulation

- Advantages
  - Active learners
  - Practice "reality" in a safe setting
  - Useful for cognitive and psychomotor domains of learning
- Limitations
  - Labor intensive
  - Costs of equipment

Factors in Selection of Instructional Methods

- What are the behavioral objectives?
- What are characteristics of the learner(s)?
- What resources are available?
- What are the teacher's strengths and limitations?

Evaluation of Instructional Methods

- Did learners achieve objectives?
- Were adequate resources available?
- Did method accommodate learner's needs, abilities, and style?

Creative Techniques to Enhance Verbal Presentations

- Enthusiasm
- Humor
- Problem-solving
- Anecdotes

General Principles for All Nurses

- Give positive reinforcement
- Exhibit acceptance/sensitivity
- Be organized, give direction
- Elicit and give feedback
- Use questioning
- Know your audience
- Summarize important points

Notes

Classification of Instructional Settings

- Healthcare setting
- Healthcare-related setting
- Non-healthcare setting

Healthcare Setting

- Definition: an organization whose primary or sole function is the delivery of health care with client education as an integral component
- Examples: hospitals, clinics, physician offices, wellness centers

Healthcare-related Setting

- Definition: a quasi-health agency whose purpose is to provide client advocacy, disseminate information, and support research on a specific health problem or issue with healthcare services as a complementary function
- Examples: American Cancer Society, Planned Parenthood of America, Head Injury support group

Non-healthcare Setting

- Definition: an organization whose primary function is the provision of a product or non-healthcare service with health care as an incidental or benefit option provided
- Examples: schools, YMCA/YWCA, senior centers, business/industry

Notes

Notes

Chapter 12

Instructional Materials

Audiovisual Materials
Print and Nonprint Media

- Definition: the tangible substances and real objects used to help communicate information necessary for learning
- Purposes: to help the nurse educator deliver a message creatively and clearly

---

Advantages of Multimedia Approach

- Increases skills, retention of information
- Stimulates learners' bodily senses
- Clarifies abstract or complex concepts
- Adds variety to teaching-learning
- Reinforces learning
- Brings realism to the experience
- Saves time and energy

General Principles of Effectiveness

- Media should:
  - Change behavior by influencing a gain in cognitive, affective, and/or psychomotor skills
  - Enhance learning—no one tool is better than another
  - Complement the instructional methods

General Principles of Effectiveness (cont'd)

- Media should (cont'd):
  - Match available financial resources
  - Be appropriate for physical environment
  - Complement learners' sensory abilities, developmental stage, educational level
  - Impart accurate, current, valid and appropriate messages
  - Add diversity and information to learning

Choosing Instructional Materials

- Major variables to consider
  - **Characteristics of the learner**
    - Physical abilities
    - Perceptual abilities
    - Literacy
    - Motivational level
    - Developmental stage
    - Learning style

Notes

Choosing Instructional Materials (cont'd)

– **Characteristics of the Task**
  • Learning domain
  • What the learner needs to know, to value, or to be able to do

– **Characteristics of the Media**
  • print
  • nonprint

Three Major Components of Instructional Materials

• **Delivery System**
  – Definition: both the physical form and the hardware used to present materials.
  – Examples of physical form and hardware
    • Videotapes with VCRs
    • Computer software with computer

Three Major Components of Instructional Materials (cont'd)

• **Content**
  – Definition: actual information shared with the learner
  – Selection criteria
    • Accuracy
    • Appropriateness for content being taught
    • Readability

Notes

Three Major Components of Instructional Materials (cont'd)

- **Presentation**
  - Definition: the form most important for selecting/developing instructional materials
  - Concrete to Abstract Continuum
    - Realia
    - Illusionary Representations
    - Symbolic Representations

Types of Instructional Materials Written Materials

- Advantages
  - Available to learner in absence of nurse
  - Widely acceptable, familiar
  - Readily available, relatively cheap
  - Convenient form
  - Learner controls rate of reading
  - Content easily altered to target specific audiences

Written Materials (cont'd)

- Disadvantages
  - Most abstract form of reality
  - Immediate feedback limited
  - Proper reading level essential for full usefulness
  - Less useful with low literate learners or visually or cognitively impaired learners
  - Inappropriate for illiterate learners

Written Materials—Commercially Prepared

- Factors to be considered
  - Who produced the item? Any input by healthcare professionals?
  - Can the item be previewed?
  - The price must be consistent with its educational value

Evaluating Printed Materials

- Nature of the audience
- Literacy level required
- Linguistic variety available
- Brevity and clarity
- Layout and appearance
- Opportunity for repetition
- Concreteness and familiarity

Demonstration Materials Displays

- Advantages
  - Fast way to attract attention, make point
  - Flexible
  - Portable
  - Reusable
  - Stimulate interest or ideas in observer
  - Can change or influence attitudes
  - Purchasable and/or can be made

Notes

Demonstration Materials Displays (cont'd)

- Disadvantages
  - Take up a lot of space
  - Time-consuming to prepare—often reused, outdated
  - May be overused
  - Unsuitable for large audiences

Demonstration Materials Displays— Posters as Popular Display Tools

- Consider:
  - Color
  - White space
  - Graphics
  - KISS principle
  - Titles/Script
  - Balance of content

Demonstration Materials Models

- Advantages
  - Useful when real object too small, too large, too expensive, unavailable, too complex
  - Allows safe practice
  - More active involvement by the learner with immediate feedback available
  - Readily available

Notes

Demonstration Materials
Models (cont'd)

- Disadvantages
  - May not be suitable for learner with poor abstraction abilities or for visually impaired
  - Some models fragile, expensive, bulky, difficult to transport
  - Cannot be observed or manipulated by more than a few learners at a time

Demonstration Materials—
Three Specific Types of Models

- Replicas
  - Examples: anatomical models, resuscitation dolls
- Analogues
  - Examples: dialysis machines, computer models
- Symbols
  - Examples: words, cartoons, formulas, sign

Audiovisual Materials

- Projection Resources
  - Movies and filmstrips
  - Overhead transparencies

Projection Resources

- Advantages
  - Most effectively used with groups
  - Especially beneficial with hearing-impaired, low-literate learners
  - Excellent media for use in teaching psychomotor skills

Projection Resources (cont'd)

- Disadvantages
  - Lack of flexibility due to static content for some forms
  - Some forms may be expensive
  - Requires darkened room for some forms
  - Requires special equipment for use

Audio Resources

- Audiotapes, Radio, CD
- Advantages
  - Widely available
  - May be especially beneficial to visually-impaired, low literate learners
  - May be listened to repeatedly
  - Most forms practical, cheap, small, portable

Audio Resources (cont'd)

- Disadvantages
  - Relies only on sense of hearing
  - Some forms may be expensive
  - Lack of opportunity for interaction between instructor and learner

Video Resources

- Purchased tapes
- Making your own videos
- **Advantages**
  - Widely used educational tool
  - Inexpensive; uses visual, auditory senses
  - Flexible for use with different audiences
  - Powerful tool for role-modeling, demonstration, teaching psychomotor skills

Video Resources (cont'd)

- **Disadvantages**
  - Viewing formats limited depending on use of Beta or VHS and size of tape
  - Some commercial products may be expensive
  - Some purchased materials may be too long or inappropriate for audience

Notes

Telecommunications Resources

- Telephones, Televisions
  - **Advantages**
    - Relatively inexpensive, widely available
  - **Disadvantages**
    - Complicated to set up interactive capability
    - Expensive to broadcast via satellite

Computer Resources

- Advantages
  - Interactive potential: quick feedback, retention
  - Potential database enormous
  - Can individualize to suit different types of learners, different pace of learning
  - Time-efficient

Computer Resources (cont'd)

- Disadvantages
  - Primary learning efficacy: cognitive domain less useful for attitude/behavior change or psychomotor skill development
  - Software and hardware expensive
  - Must be purchased
  - Limited use for most elderly, low-literate learners, those with physical limitations

Evaluation Criteria for Selecting Materials

- Considerations
  - Learner
  - Task
  - Media available
- Evaluation Checklist
  - Content
  - Instructional design
  - Technical production
  - Packaging

Notes

_____
_____
_____
_____
_____
_____
_____
_____
_____
_____
_____
_____
_____
_____
_____
_____
_____
_____
_____
_____
_____
_____
_____
_____
_____
_____
_____
_____
_____
_____
_____
_____
_____
_____

Chapter 13

Technology in Education

The Information Age

- A period in history characterized by
  - Growth of technology
  - Information explosion

The Information Age

- Impact on teachers and learners:
  - Learning has become a shared responsibility
  - Teacher has taken on the role of facilitator

The Information Age

- Impact of Information Age technology on education:
  - Greater access to educational programs
  - Access to a world-wide audience
  - Interactive learning opportunities

The Information Age

- Trends:
  - Establishment of standards
    - e-Health Code of Ethics
    - Criteria for evaluating Web sites
  - Development of new field of study
    - Consumer Informatics

E-Health Code of Ethics

- Candor
- Honesty
- Quality
- Informed Consent
- Privacy
- Professionalism

E-Health Code of Ethics (cont'd)

- Responsible partnering
- Accountability

Criteria for Evaluating Web Sites

- Accuracy
- Design
- Authors/Sponsors
- Currency
- Authority

Consumer Informatics

- Analyzes consumer needs for information
- Studies/implements methods for making information accessible
- Models/integrates consumer preferences into medical information systems

Notes

On-line Healthcare Education

- World Wide Web (WWW)
- Internet

World Wide Web (WWW)

- "Virtual Space" for information
- Component of the Internet
- >1,000,000,000 Web pages
- Text, graphics, audio & video
- Released in 1989

Health Information on the WWW

- Designed for consumers and healthcare professionals
- Averages over 22,000,000 hits/month
- Used by over 52,000,000 Americans per month
- Wide range of sites providing a variety of services and types of information

Pew Report on Web Use

- Approximately 21 million Americans have used Web information to:
  - Make decisions about how to treat an illness
  - Decide whether or not to seek a health care provider
  - Identify questions to be answered
  - Decide to seek a second opinion

Nurse Educators and the WWW

- Recognizing the influence of the WWW nurses should:
  - Assess client's use of the WWW
  - Clarify information found by clients
  - Share resources
  - Create Web-based resources
  - Teach information literacy skills

Computer Literacy

- The ability to use the computer hardware and software necessary to accomplish routine tasks

Information Literacy

- The ability to:
  - Access needed information
  - Evaluate information found
  - Organize information
  - Use information from a variety of sources

Information Literacy Skills for Web Use

- Ability to:
  - Reduce a problem to a searchable command
  - Categorize a Web page according to its purpose
  - Identify sources of potential bias
  - Make judgments about accuracy and reliability of information found

Information Literacy Skills for Web Use (cont'd)

- The ability to:
  - Make decisions about comprehensiveness of information found
  - Determine currency

Information Literacy Skills for Web Use (cont'd)

- The ability to:
  - Identify resources to answer questions or verify assumptions made

E-Mail

- Advantages:
  - Easy to use
  - Can be used any time day or night
  - Low cost
  - World-wide
  - Provides a written record

E-mail

- Disadvantages:
  - Messages lack context
  - Takes time to complete an interaction
  - Legal issues related to the written record created
  - Privacy cannot be assured

Electronic Discussion Groups

- Broad category covering many formats of on-line discussion.
- Advantages:
  - Means of networking
  - Vehicle for information exchange
  - Can be used to provide on-line support
  - Easy to use
  - Low cost
  - Anonymity

Electronic Discussion Groups

- Disadvantages:
  - Few checks for accuracy
  - Can be time consuming
  - May result in e-mail overload

Chat Rooms

- Advantages:
  - Allows for real time discussion
  - Widely accessible
  - Provides a mechanism for information exchange

Chat Rooms

- Disadvantages:
  - Moves very quickly
  - May be difficult to follow
  - Requires everyone to be on a the same time

Digital Divide

- The gap between those individuals who have access to information technology resources and those who do not

Digital Divide

- Risk factors:
  - Age (>65 years)
  - Income (<$35,000/year household income)
  - Race/ethnic origin ((african america, hispanic)
  - Level of education (<high school)
  - Ability (presence of disability)

Interventions with Older Adults

- Teach principles of ergonomics
- Provide access to resources
- Use motivational strategies
- Create non-threatening teaching environments

Promoting Digital Inclusion for People with Disabilities

- Web page design
- Software selection
- Adaptive Devices

Working with Groups at Risk

- Recognize/assess risk factors
- Be knowledgeable about resources
- Create supportive environments

Professional Education

- Degree programs for distance learners are increasingly available
- Continued education programs are widely available in a variety of formats
- Staff development and training via technology is increasing

Degree Programs

- Distance Programs offered at all levels
- Accredited by NLNAC and/or CCNE
- Increased use of on-line format
- Standards for quality in distance education have been developed

E-Learning

- "Just in time training"
- "Any time ... any where"
- Designed for convenience and functionality

Summary

- Technology is a powerful tool to enhance learning. However, technology is a means to an end, not an end in and of itself. It must be used with thought, careful planning, and thorough evaluation.

Notes

Chapter 14

Evaluation in Health-Care Education

Evaluation…

- A process
- A critical component of other processes
  - Nursing process
  - Decision-making process
  - Education process
- Can provide data to demonstrate effectiveness
- The bridge at the end of one process that guides direction of the next

Definition of Evaluation

- Evaluation: A systematic and continuous process by which the significance or worth of something is judged; the process of collecting and using information to determine what has been accomplished and how well it has been accomplished to guide decision making.

Steps in Evaluation

- Focus
- Design
- Conduct
- Analyze
- Interpret
- Report
- Use

Evaluation

- Assessment = Input
- Evaluation = Output

The Difference Between Assessment and Evaluation

- Assessment and evaluation are two concepts that are highly inter-related and are often used interchangeably as terms, but they are not synonymous.
- Assessment: a process to gather, summarize, interpret, and use data to decide a direction for action.
- Evaluation: a process to gather, summarize, interpret, and use data to determine the extent to which an action was successful.

Five Foci of Evaluation

- In planning any evaluation, the first and most crucial step is to determine the focus of the evaluation.
- Evaluation focus includes five basic components:
  - Audience
  - Purpose
  - Questions
  - Scope
  - Resources

Evaluation Focus

- To determine these components, the following five questions should be asked:
  - For what **audience** is the evaluation being conducted?
  - For what **purpose** is the evaluation being conducted?
  - What **questions** will be asked?
  - What is the **scope** of the evaluation?
  - What **resources** are available to conduct the evaluation?

RSA Evaluation Model

high — low

time & cost — frequency

Impact
Outcome
Content
Process
Total Program

low — high

Notes

Process (Formative) Evaluation

- **Audience:** individual educator
- **Purpose:** to make adjustments as soon as needed during education process
- **Question:** What can better facilitate learning?
- **Scope:** limited to specific learning experience; frequent; concurrent with learning
- **Resources:** inexpensive & available

Content Evaluation

- **Audience:** educator/clinician individual or team
- **Purpose:** to determine if learners have acquired knowledge/skills just taught
- **Question:** To what degree did learners achieve specified objectives?
- **Scope:** limited to specific learning experience & objectives; immediately after education completed (short-term)
- **Resources:** relatively inexpensive; available

Outcome (Summative) Evaluation

- **Audience:** educator, education team/ director, education funding group
- **Purpose:** to determine effects of teaching
- **Question:** Were goals met? Did (planned) change in behaviors occur?
- **Scope:** broader scope, more long term & less frequent than content evaluation
- **Resources:** expensive, sophisticated, may require expertise less readily available

Impact Evaluation

- **Audience:** institution administration, funding agency, community
- **Purpose:** to determine relative effects of education on institution or community
- **Question:** What is the effect of education on long-term changes at the organizational or community level
- **Scope:** broad, complex, sophisticated, long-term; occurs infrequently
- **Resources:** extensive, resource-intensive

Total Program Evaluation

- **Audience:** education dept, institutional administration, funding agency, community
- **Purpose:** to determine extent to which total program meets/exceeds long-term goals
- **Question:** To what extent did all program activities meet annual departmental/ institutional/community goals?
- **Scope:** broad, long-term/strategic; lengthy therefore conducted infrequently
- **Resources:** extensive, resource-intensive

Evaluation vs. Research

- Audience specific to single person, group, institution, or location
- Conducted to make decisions in specific setting
- Focused on needs of primary audience
- Time constrained by urgency of decisions to be made

- Audience generic
- Conducted to generate new knowledge and/or expand existing knowledge
- Focused on sample representativeness, generalizability of findings
- Time constrained by study funding

Five Levels of Learner Evaluation

LEVEL 0	LEVEL I	LEVEL II	LEVEL III	LEVEL IV
Learner's dis-satisfaction & readiness to learn	Learner's par-ticipation & satisfaction during inter-vention	Learner's per-formance & satisfaction after interven-tion	Learner's per-formance & attitude in daily setting	Learner's maintained performance & attitude
(Needs assessment)	(Initial; process)	(Short-term; content)	(Long-term; outcome)	(Ongoing; impact)

Evaluation Methods

- **What types of data will be collected?**
  - Complete (people, program, environment)
  - Concise (will answer evaluation questions)
  - Clear (use operational definitions)
  - Comprehensive (quantitative & qualitative)
- **From whom or what will data be collected?**
  - From participants, surrogates, documents, and/or pre-existing databases
  - Include population or sample

Evaluation Methods (cont'd)

- **How, when, and where will data be collected?**
  - By observation, interview, questionnaire, test, record review, secondary analysis
  - Consistent with type of evaluation
  - Consistent with questions to be answered
- **By whom will data be collected?**
  - By learner, educator, evaluator, and/or trained data collector
  - Select to minimize bias

Notes

Selecting an Evaluation Instrument

- Identify existing instruments through literature search, review of similar evaluations conducted in the past
- Critique potential instruments for:
  - Fit with definitions of factors to be measured
  - Evidence of reliability & validity, especially with a similar population
  - Appropriateness for those being evaluated
  - Affordability, feasibility

Evaluation Barriers

- Lack of clarity
  - Resolve by clearly describing 5 evaluation components
  - Specify and operationally define terms
- Lack of ability
  - Resolve by making necessary resources available
  - Solicit support from experts

Evaluation Barriers (cont'd)

- Fear of punishment or loss of self-esteem
  - Resolve by being aware of existence of fear among those being evaluated
  - Focus on data and results without personalizing or blaming
  - Point out achievements
  - Encourage ongoing effort
  - COMMUNICATE!!!

Notes

When conducting an evaluation…

- Conduct a pilot test first
  - Assess feasibility of conducting the full evaluation as planned
  - Assess reliability, validity of instruments
- Include "extra" time
  - Be prepared for unexpected delays
- Keep a sense of humor!

Data Analysis and Interpretation

- The purpose for conducting data analysis are two-fold:
  1. To organize data so that they can provide meaningful information, such as through the use of tables and graphs.
  2. To provide answers to evaluation questions.
- Data can be quantitative and/or qualitative in nature.

Reporting Evaluation Results

- Be audience focused
  - Begin with a one-page executive summary
  - Use format & language clear to the audience
  - Present results in person and in writing
  - Provide specific recommendations
- Stick to the evaluation purpose
  - Directly answer questions asked

Reporting Evaluation Results (cont'd)

- Stick to the data
  - Maintain consistency between results and interpretation of results
  - Identify limitations

Summary of Evaluation Process

- The process of evaluation in health-care education is to gather, summarize, interpret, and use data to determine the extent to which an educational activity is efficient, effective, and useful to learners, teachers and sponsors.
- Each aspect of the evaluation process is important, but all of them are meaningless unless the results of evaluation are used to guide future action in planning and carrying out interventions.

Notes